As Far As
You Can Go
Without
a Passport

*The View from the End
of the Road*

As Far As You Can Go Without a Passport

The View From the End of the Road

Comments and Comic Pieces
by
TOM BODETT

ADDISON-WESLEY PUBLISHING COMPANY, INC.

Reading, Massachusetts   Menlo Park, California
Don Mills, Ontario   Wokingham, England   Amsterdam
Sydney   Singapore   Tokyo   Mexico City   Bogotá   Santiago
San Juan

Different versions of many of these pieces were aired over National Public Radio's "All Things Considered" between late 1984 and 1985.

Many of the designations used by manufacturers and sellers to distinguish their products are claimed as trademarks. Where those designations appear in this book and Addison-Wesley was aware of a trademark claim, the designations have been printed in initial caps (i.e., Life Savers).

Library of Congress Cataloging-in-Publication Data

Bodett, Tom.
  As far as you can go without a passport.

  1. Alaska—Social life and customs—Addresses, essays, lectures. 2. Bodett, Tom—Addresses, essays, lectures.
I. Title.
F910.5.B63   1985   306'.09798   85-13478
ISBN 0-201-10661-2

Cover illustration by Alfred Ramage
Cover design by Marshall Henrichs
Text design by Anna Post
Set in 11-point ITC Garamond Book by Compset Inc., Beverly, MA

ABCDEFGHIJK-DO-898765
First printing, August 1985

To Courtney.
May you grow into a reasonable man.

ACKNOWLEDGMENTS

First, I offer many thanks to the entire staff at radio station KBBI in Homer, Alaska, for their unfailing support and the use of their facilities. I also thank my friends and colleagues at National Public Radio's "All Things Considered" — I thank them all for their genuine interest and endless patience with my steady barrage of toll-free telephone calls.

I'd also like to thank my editor at Addison-Wesley, Robert Lavelle, and the entire General Publishing Division staff for making this undertaking such a pleasant experience. Their support and enthusiasm is much appreciated.

Finally, I'd like to thank my wife, Debi. This book was completed at about the same time that she gave birth to our son, Courtney. Her graceful accomplishment has put this small project in perspective. I thank her for her encouragement, love, and the constant source of inspiration she proved herself to be throughout the writing of this collection.

Contents

As Far As
You Can Go
Without
a Passport

*The View from the End
of the Road*

Introduction

I'D LIKE to be able to say that this collection was an inspired concept planted during my college days in Michigan and cultivated by ten years of association with loggers, fishermen, barflies, and ne'er-do-wells in and around Alaska. But if I'm to be honest, I must admit that college had very little to do with it.

I started writing little ditties for our local public radio station sometime in the spring of 1984. It was good fun for all and served the purpose of busying up a typically sluggish Monday-morning news format. My only gift being an incredibly average existence, folks brought me into their hearts and homes as "one of their own." It was just a matter of months before I was finally prodded by the local staff to submit my commentaries to National Public Radio's news program, "All Things Considered." To my surprise and immeasurable delight, they were accepted for broadcast, and my work has been heard all over the place on a

1

regular basis since then. Reaction has always been the same. "I know what you mean" pretty much sums up the mail I get. One listener from the South wrote that "it's nice to hear a voice that is not just another cliché-ridden quiche-eater." Impressive.

Although I may not be *ridden* with clichés, I'm quite susceptible to them, and he was right about my aversion to quiche, also an eighties cliché for limp wrists, soft politics, and love of bottled waters. My wife makes a wonderful quiche, but I'm so aware of its dubious image that even her flaky crust cannot overcome this unappetizing mystique. Remember, this is Alaska, where machismo is an epidemic and hating every poet but Robert Service is considered an Arctic survival skill.

Sometime after my debut on National Public Radio I got this call from a Boston publisher that wanted me to send everything I had to them for consideration as a book. Right. Happens every day, I suppose. House builders who write evenings and weekends all over the country get offers from publishing houses, don't they? To make a small-town-boy-does-good story short, Addison-Wesley Publishing Company sent me a nice check with instructions to "take the winter off and write us a book of this stuff." No problem.

Putting my winter construction schedule off until spring, I went about the chore of converting my "office" into a "study." This consisted mainly of replacing the *Uniform Building Code* on my desk with *Webster's New World Dictionary,* letting all my blueprints fall behind the drier, and dragging my portable air compressor closer to the chair to prop my feet on. My editor will attest to the vague smell of chain-saw gas about my manuscript submissions.

I bought a new typewriter that knows more than I do and tried to start thinking like an author. Nothing to it. All the pleasantry I once contributed as my share of a tavern tirade on truth and beauty, or a snowbound reflection with good friends, went instead through my smarter Brother typewriter, on to Boston, and into this book.

It's a pretty normal book about pretty normal things, and needs little introduction outside of my certifying that the author is a pretty normal guy. I don't think it happens very often that a writer is able to have his work published without first being assaulted by a barrage of rejections and a stiff climb up the mind-grinder, which can be the literary ladder of success. I was very lucky and caught the express elevator. In that way, the reader is getting what might be a "fresh" bit of work. Whether fresh in its voice and outlook or simply in its naiveté, I'll leave for you to decide. It is composed of the honest thoughts of a fortunate man who lives a reasonably honorable life in a far-flung corner of America.

Acknowledgment should go to a near-fatal accident suffered ten years ago, which gave me the wild hair to come to this great state in the first place, and to all those incredible people I've lived with, worked with, fought, cried, and drank with along the way since then.

Alaska is one of the sanest places in the world. At once demanding and acceptant, always irreverent, and seldom monotonous. A place where I'm proud to live, full of people I'm proud to know. I've borrowed from them all unmercifully, and if the reader should derive any pleasure whatsoever from this collection of my thoughts and anecdotes, it is a credit to all of us here at the end of the road.

PART
1

AT HOME

The End
of the Road

IT SEEMS LIKE every town you come to, big or small, has got something unique about it. Something it's *best* at.

I grew up in a little town in southern Michigan, Sturgis. I'll bet you never heard of it. No reason why you should. It's on U. S. 12 about halfway between Detroit and Chicago on the Michigan side of the Michigan-Indiana border by a mile and a half. Being in Michigan doesn't account for a whole lot, and being near Indiana is worth a whole lot less. But what this little burg does have all to its own is the headquarters of the largest curtain rod manufacturer in the world. Kirsch. You've heard of that, right? Did you ever read the box? Says "Sturgis, Michigan" all over it. She's the Curtain Rod Capital of the World, you bet. Says so right on the sign coming into town. At least it used to. Right below the Rotary Club and Lions emblems. When you rolled by that sign, you knew you were someplace.

7

My Mom grew up in Kewanee, Illinois. Never heard of that either, I suppose. It's just a pleasant little antique town nestled into the endless cornfields of central Illinois. What could possibly be special about Kewanee? You could have had a little piece of it for breakfast this morning with your eggs. Kewanee, Illinois, is the Hog Capital of America. They sell a lot of pigs there. More than anybody, by the sounds of it. It makes them significant. Helps those that live there live just a little better, maybe.

A lot of places have stuff like that. Fort Wayne, Indiana: Home of the Largest Chevrolet Dealer in the Midwest. Smoky Gary is our steel capital on the lakes. Then there's the Windy City; lotsa wind in Chicago. Omaha's got the insurance. Otherwise uninteresting enterprises reach for notoriety with grand names and questionable claims. There's Seashell Cities on the landlocked plains. Wall Drug, world's largest drugstore and petrified watermelon patch. Out in jackelope land there's Little America, largest filling station in the world. One hundred and eighty pumps the last time I was through there. Very impressive.

There's corn capitals, artichoke capitals, lumber, shipping, fishing, and on and on through Alaska right to the very end of the road, and that's us. So what's that make us — Turnaround Capital of America? I don't know, but this is where America stops, carwise. If you got into your car in New York and wanted to take a nice long drive, I mean the *longest* drive you could without turning around or running into a foreign language, this is where you'd wind up. You can get west of here if you want to, but you've got to leave your car with us. Homer, Alaska, the end of the road.

What a nice ending it is too.

If Hollywood were to stage a highway ending extravaganza, this is how they'd do it. It doesn't just get to the beach and stop. There's a real drama to it. You'll crest over the hill just before Homer and look over a misty bay right out of Greek mythology. You can see the end of the road from there. It rides the back of a natural gravel bar some five miles into the bay and just stops. You get out of your car and find yourself in the parking lot of a bar and restaurant surrounded by three hundred and sixty degrees of the prettiest country in the world.

Now that's the way to end a road. No sign. No park with a brass plaque, souvenir stand, and pay telescope. Just a dirt parking lot with a puddle in it, a decent bar, and the feeling like you really got to someplace. As far as ends of roads go, I'd give it a "ten"; of course, I never seen the other end. Or would it be the beginning? All in how you look at it, I guess.

If you were born in Homer, this might be the beginning of the road, but if you were from the Curtain Rod Capital of the World, this would be as far away as you could get without a good boat and a passport.

A lotta folks drift in here, I think, because they haven't found what they wanted yet and this is where they've gotta stop.

They could've done worse.

There's warmer places. There's richer places. There may even be a prettier place or two out there. But the longer one stays at the end of the road, the easier it is not to look back up it in search for someplace better.

It may be to our credit, and it might be the death of us, but there is no turnaround at the end of the road.

Sleep Guilt

IT'S A SLEEPY TIME of year around Alaska. The weather's lousy, work is slow, and the money's about as short as the days are. It's just plain hard to get out of bed in the morning. My wife is usually up and out of the house by seven-thirty or so. This leaves me to lie there and contemplate the implications of rising before dawn. They're all bad, and more times than not I abandon the thought and dig in for a good old-fashioned snooze.

It never matters which day of the week I decide to sleep in on. There's always a friend of mine or someone who got up exceptionally early and wants everyone to know about it. So the phone rings, and rings, and rings some more. When I finally pick it up, yawning and scratching, they always have to ask with a snicker, "Did I get you up?" Then something happens inside of me that I can't control. A wave of self-righteous indignation sweeps over me.

I puff out my chest, clear my throat, and *lie* right through my teeth. "No," I say, "I was just in the shower rinsing off from my morning run." Or, "Heck no. I was changing the oil in my truck and you caught me underneath the thing." I don't know if they buy it or not, but they always apologize and decide to call back when I'm not so busy.

I go back to bed and lie there, wide awake. My heart pounds and my body aches with that one awful hindrance of late sleepers everywhere: that nagging sensation that you should be doing something other than punching the snooze button and listening to your stomach gurgle. I hate that feeling because I can't control it, and I'm not even sure where it comes from.

It's not like I sleep twelve hours a day or anything. I take my eight like everyone else. I just take it a little later this time of year. I stay up at night to take advantage of the boundless cultural affairs the winter has to offer. Like watching a classic old late movie with an all-star cast. Well, actually, it was a disaster-movie rerun with rich, beautiful women in spiked heels climbing through the wreckage of a big-city subway system. Or was it an upside-down luxury cruise ship? I really don't remember, but it was good, and now I'm tired and need the sleep.

I lie there and try to block from my mind the unmistakable sounds of a new day dawning. The neighbor's rooster crows. The magpies sit outside my window calling me obscene names in some horrible bird language. Then someone starts showing off with a chain saw about a half-mile from here. The dog begins bouncing off the front door, and finally, after about my twenty-fifth whack on the snooze button, I'm up — fresh, fit, and sunny as an old, sick bear. I stand in the shower having an endurance contest with the hot-water heater and vow to get to bed at a decent hour for a change. But I never do. Not this time of year.

I'm in my winter mode, and I'll sleep until ten with pride, thank you. If you overachievers out there want to early-to-bed and early-to-rise yourselves through the dark months, that's up to you. Just don't go calling at the crack of dawn to inflict your puritanical values on me. I'm entirely at ease with my sleeping habits and don't need you calling to bug me. Besides, you'll never get the satisfaction of waking me up 'cause I'm going to lie to you anyway.

The Sock
Conspiracy

I KNOW we've all heard a lot about sock behavior and the persistent habit they have of disappearing in the laundry. Philosophers, ministers, and stand-up comics have discoursed on the subject for years, but there're never any answers, only more jokes and nervous laughter. Why isn't someone addressing this issue? People, we have a problem here. We're resigning ourselves to this much too easily. You ask your wife, "Honey, where's my other blue sock?"

"It was lost in the wash," she says.

"Oh, I see."

What do you mean, you see? It makes as much sense as saying the Martians came and got it. Where is that sock? You look in the drier lint screen and there's a ball of fuzz, all right, but not a sock's worth. Look in the washer filter and there's some more wet fuzz, but the two together aren't enough to make a nose-warmer. This is an all too familiar household story, right?

Home products manufacturers have thus far met with every challenge. Problem stains, dull floors, and dishpan hands are all a thing of the past. Scratchy toilet paper, all but obsolete, can only be found in cheap gas-station rest rooms. They make exhaust vents for smells, thermostats to regulate everything, timers for lights, and central vacuum systems, but they can't keep the laundry from eating your socks. Or can they? This reeks of conspiracy. I don't think they're telling us everything they know about driers.

We're talking big money here. If everyone who ever lost a sock to the wash had kept a record of it, can you imagine the figures we'd be looking at? Truckload upon truckload of mismatched socks are unaccounted for. The dollar value of missing socks in America alone last year would be equal to the gross national product of many Third World nations.

Who's behind this and what do they want? Could the garment and appliance industries be in cahoots together, creating an artificial sock demand to keep us buying? Are they buying up patents on sock-safe dryers to keep them under wraps? Imagine the impact on the sock market were Sears to come out with a washer-drier combo that didn't vaporize knitted footwear.

So you can see what we're up against here. It's big. I'm working on it, but in the meantime, I'd wash 'em in the sink and dry 'em by the stove. Just keep your eye on them.

Grocery Shopping

I USUALLY SHOP for groceries with a list. Easy enough to do. Walk around, item by item, get what you need, and get the heck out of there. But my house partner, wife, and list provider left a month ago on vacation, and I'm just now beginning to realize what a drag shopping for groceries can really be. Especially if you don't know the rules.

There is one unbending truth I've begun to grasp. Never, ever go into a grocery store without a list. This should be taught in schools. Also keep in mind that if you should find yourself needing a grocery store without a list at hand, be sure to eat something before you go in. Not having been blessed with this higher education, I had to learn the hard way.

The first mistake is made at the door. You're hungry and in a hurry, so you don't take a cart when you walk in.

You should always take a cart when shopping for groceries without a list even if all you came in for was razor blades. On your way to get that single item you came for, you pass, say, the meat counter. There's a big ol' steak marked down for quick sale 'cause it's getting a little ripe, but not near as ripe as those ballpark franks you were headed home to eat for the tenth time; so you tuck that up under your arm. That'll sure be a nice treat, but you can't remember if you have any steak sauce or not, so you grab a little bottle of that just in case. You're beginning to salivate at this point and are easy prey for any food item your eyes might focus on. A sane person would now beat a hasty retreat to the checkout, but if you're like me, you'll just blunder on into the store's darkest reaches.

Well, a guy's gotta have a salad and a potato to enjoy a good steak, so you zip into the produce section for a head of lettuce and a spud. Twenty minutes later you stagger back out in a crouch with a head of lettuce wedged under your arm next to that steak. Between the fingers of one hand you carry the little bottle of steak sauce, a baggie full of mushrooms, two carrots, a green pepper stuck on the end of your little finger, and a can of smoked oysters you picked up on the way in. You've forgotten the potato, but instead are palming a nice plump cantaloupe in the free hand. Can't eat a meal like that without a dessert, now, can you? Speaking of desserts, you haven't tasted any of that Häagen-Dazs walnut-chip ice cream in a long time; so lets just swing through the frozen foods on the way out.

You've made it to the checkout line. Your back is stooped, your fingers are asleep, and you have to keep juggling the carton of ice cream from the crook of one arm to the other to keep from getting frost-bit. This disturbs the meat package, which drips red juice down your side the whole time you watch the lady in front of you check through a full cart of groceries. She waits until the end to start writing out her check and then gets into a five-minute argument with the clerk over the total sale. This whole time you can't wait to set some stuff down so you can pick up a couple of Hershey bars that are right in front of your nose. Gotta have something for the ride home.

Twenty bucks later you're back on the street, none the wiser. Its not until the middle of the night, when a bad dream wakes you to a prize heartburn from eating all that stuff, that you realize you forgot the milk. You pull out a pad and go to write it down, but realize that your fingers are all twisted and sore and won't negotiate the pencil.

"Aw, the heck with it," you say, "who needs a list? I'll just stop on the way home tomorrow and pick up the milk."

Bon Appétit

WHAT WITH MY WIFE be-
ing in a rather advanced stage of pregnancy, I thought it
was about time I started doing my share of the cooking
around here. In seven years of marriage my culinary spe-
cialties have only amounted to steaks, most of your basic
grill items, and your occasional boiled potato, with skin.
That's what I like to eat, so that's what I always cooked. It
was seldom varied and got a little tiresome to all involved.

I've changed all that recently by finally recognizing
the potential of cookbooks. There's a whole pile of them
in the kitchen, but they've always been a sort of wish book
for me. I'd leaf through them every so often just to whet
my appetite, then I'd throw another steak on the grill and
boil some more potatoes. I finally got to reading one of
them buggers, and by golly, it sounded easy, so I tried one.
It was a little spiral-bound job with full-color pictures of

assorted Oriental dishes. Always being a sucker for Chinese food, I started thumbing through it and found a pretty good-looking dish there called Celery Beef. I chose it over the others as it had the shortest list of ingredients, and the main one, being a cheap piece of beef rump, was quite handily thawing on the kitchen counter at that very minute.

The rest of the components were fairly elementary: celery, of course, soy sauce (lots of that), some vinegar, green onions, and garlic. The only two that threw me were the dry sherry and the ginger root. I didn't sweat the sherry. We had a bottle of old Mogen David 20-20 someone had left at the house a couple years ago, and I figured cheap beef wouldn't know the difference. But that ginger root had me worried. I'd seen it, of course, lying mysteriously between the mushrooms and green peppers like some kind of mutated sweet potato. Little sign above it in the produce section told me it was what I wanted, but how do you know a good ginger root when you see one? Remembering my cantaloupe and tomato training, I squeezed and poked at them, but didn't seem to be finding anything out. Thus utilizing my number-one rule of shopping — *when in doubt, get a big one* — I did, and headed home to concoct this textbook delight.

We have this big red wok you could fry a good-sized dog in. I dragged it out of the closet, blew the dust off it, and rolled up my sleeves. I read through the recipe and, step by tasty step, worked my way toward dinner. Just like playing with a chemistry set.

A tablespoon of this, a dash of that, stir-fry for three minutes, drain and store and cook some more. What fun. When the kitchen started to smell like the alley behind the

Wong Chow Chinese-American Café, I knew I had something going. Every place the book called for sherry, I poured in three times the amount of the MD 20-20, thinking that the old cheap wine wouldn't hold its flavor as well as the good stuff.

My wife came home, caught a whiff, and thought she had the wrong house. I was grinning like a fool and tossing celery around that wok like there was no tomorrow. She made the suggestion that if I slowed my stir some and let the food hit the pan, it might actually cook.

I poured in the last ingredient, pushed it around some, and pretty soon it looked like, well, *food*. Oriental food at that. I poured the whole works over some rice I'd been fussing with this whole time and took stock of my accomplishment. "Looks too good to eat," I said, holding up the cookbook behind my plate. "See, just like the picture."

I could tell she liked it because every time she bit into a hunk of that ginger root, tears would come to her eyes and she'd look over at me and smile. Boy, was I pleased. Her only complaint was that several hours later she thought her mouth held the unmistakable aftertaste of a wino's overcoat. "Nothing to worry about," I told her. "That's all part of gourmet cooking."

So I tried the Beef Chow Mein last night, and the Hot Chili Chinese Chicken the night before that. I notice my wife walks more slowly from the car to the house these days, and with a vague air of caution about her. I don't know, I must be feeding her too good.

Small Places

My WIFE AND I have lived in small houses so long you'd think we'd be used to it by now. But it never fails. Every year we drift a little closer to flipping out for good. We try to prevent it. We have some rules that only people living in small places could understand.

Only one person can get out of bed at a time in the morning. First one up has to be completely showered, dressed, and fed before the other is allowed out of bed. It's a harsh rule, I know, but it works; and besides, I'm never the first one up. Another rule is no unnecessary motion. If you need something, the odds are that the other person can reach it from where they're sitting and just hand it to you. So just ask for it.

I think this rule started when we began letting the dog in the house. If you stand up, the dog stands up, wags his tail, and knocks over somebody's orange juice. There's a big mess, everybody gets upset, and the dog sleeps outside again. So it's best just to stay calm and try not to move around a lot.

We've lived together long enough that motion in itself is not a big problem. We're like magnets that repel each other in one of those little maze games. She starts down the hall; I back out. I go for a cup of coffee; she sidesteps to the sink, and not a word is said. Those are the good days. The bad days are when you open up the cupboard to get a glass, the spaghetti bag opens and dumps those sharp and stiff little noodles all over your bare feet, and then they break on the rug. The vacuum cleaner is buried under the cat food, laundry soap, and a clothes basket — requiring what amounts to a minor archaeological dig to uncover it. Those are the days when the neighborhood is treated to a helpless scream of sorts and one of us stomps out of the house for a walk or a drive.

In the winter even a drive in the country can be a confining and maddening experience. Compact cars and trucks should not be sold in the same states as insulated pack boots. You can push down all three pedals with one foot. This will simultaneously accelerate, break, and drop the vehicle out of gear, effectively red-lining the engine. Then you panic, lift your foot, and neatly stall the car with a lurch into traffic. The whole time, you're trying to scrape a little peephole in the frost on your windshield. It's enough to drive you to strange religions.

If they promised a heaven where gas was thirty-two cents a gallon and all they sold were Buicks, I'd be a re-formed man. But instead they keep selling us smaller and smaller cars to drive us around between smaller and smaller houses. I know I shouldn't let it get me down.

One positive aspect of living in a small place is that we can adequately heat our home with a good conversation and a mood candle. If it does get a little stuffy, opening the door for fifteen seconds will give us a complete air exchange. The only problem is that the exchanged air is never quite as warm as the old, so we don't do that very often and have a tendency to sometimes smell like what we had for dinner the night before.

All in all it's not so bad, and like good Americans we sit fat and happy, and try not to think about it. It keeps us close and promotes togetherness, much in the same way prisoner-of-war camps do. Although I'm certain that keeping two prisoners in a cell the size of our house would be a violation of the Geneva Convention, we call it home, and like everybody's home it's almost always the best place to be.

PART
2

SEASONS

Cutting
Trees

I HAD A LITTLE FUN over the weekend. My wife and I decided once and for all to do the addition onto the house, and there were two trees that just had to go. We weighed the pros and cons, filed a little environmental impact statement with ourselves, and decided that, nope, we didn't want two trees in the living room.

There is some perverted joy I get out of cutting trees. I've never quite figured out exactly what it is, but there's nothing like reducing a half-century-old black spruce to a pile of eighteen-inch fire logs. I'm sure this must be some form of neurosis that should be studied, if it hasn't been already. It must go back to early childhood — like stomping the crap out of every anthill you see, throwing rocks at birds, killing grass snakes, that sort of thing. Kick ol' Mother Nature in the shins every once in a while just to let her know you're something to be reckoned with. I think it's natural. At least I hope so; sure is fun.

I tackled those trees with the flare and grim purpose you get when starting a chain saw. Spurred by the self-righteousness that comes with breaking a sweat on Sunday. We soon had them lying side by side on the ground more or less exactly where we wanted them. I dropped them dead in between the doghouse and front porch, and felt awful proud of myself as I squinted through the blue chain-saw smoke. You wouldn't appreciate that accomplishment as much if you knew that our doghouse and front porch are seventy-five feet apart, and that the trees weren't long enough to reach either one of them anyway. But I must have looked grand standing there in the smoky haze, one foot up on a stump and the saw balanced on my knee. You see, I don't do this very often, and chain saws are great for striking poses with.

We went to work with ax and saw, stripped the trees of their limbs, bucked them into woodstove size, and hauled the branches to the landfill. By the time I got back, my wife had all the loose debris raked up, the wood stacked, and there was nothing left of those trees but a big empty place and two stumps. Our adrenaline still pumping from a job well done, we attacked the stumps with shovel and ax in a flurry of sweat and grunts. Forty-five minutes later we'd cut every possible connection between those two stumps and planet Earth, but they wouldn't move an inch. It was beginning to dawn on me that those trees were not going to give up without a fight. Undaunted, we laid in a second siege with shovel and ax and pee-vee and come-along, and chain, and an old Ford pickup, and some words I can't commit to print, and by God, pretty soon we got one to lean over a little bit. It wasn't leaning near as much as the two of us were by then. We were beginning to think that two nice trees like that wouldn't have looked too bad in the new living room after all.

We decided that we shouldn't have all the fun in one weekend and we'd save the stump battle for next week. We'll get 'em yet. We're Americans, by God, and Alaskans to boot. Hard work and ingenuity coupled with the fortitude of pioneers will make short work of what's left of those two trees. Individual man against his environment. That's the spirit that built this country, and that's the spirit that'll pull those stumps.

Of course, that and the back hoe I'm going to dig the foundation with next weekend.

The End
of Summer

THERE'S SURE NO such thing as long, dull summers on Alaska's Kenai Peninsula. In fact, a person has to be pretty quick-witted to see it at all. I missed it this year somehow. Things started greening up real nice in May, and I felt myself revitalizing and making mental and practical plans for the summer. Everything from retaining walls over the driveway to late-night volley-ball extravaganzas with good friends was scheduled and anticipated. Of course, work picked up and we got busy, as did our friends. About the same time we reached the peak of our energy, I saw that the fireweed had also peaked. They say you've got six weeks to the first snowfall from the time the fireweed turns color, and that it's doing. Oh boy, six weeks. So now we eye the stuff suspiciously and feel just a little better when we see a few late bloomers here and there. All the neat little things we were going to do over the summer have been replaced by all the dirty little jobs that have to be done before winter. Where did the time go? I think there must be a thirty- or forty-minute period between the time the grass turns green and when it starts turning brown again. That's our summer, and I missed it. It seems like just a couple of weeks ago I was wishing a few fishing buddies good catches, and here they're back already recounting their seasons to me. How about that volleyball game we never got to? Well, they would, but they've just got to get that water line buried to the house before snow flies, and they have to start thinking about getting the boat put up. God, I don't even have the roof put on the addition yet. The pipes are sure to freeze if I don't get that thing skirted. The fleeting smile of summer is suddenly the set jaws of fall and winter. Oh well. It keeps us on our toes anyway.

Even our goofing-off days resemble activity. We take a couple of days off to go fishing, take a drive to Anchorage, maybe get some building material while we're there. Then there's the granddaddy goof-off of them all: moose hunting, deer hunting, goose, duck, goat. God, it's endless. We work harder on our days off than otherwise. There's virtue in that somehow. Alaskans should be proud of that. Sure, we miss the summers we never seem to get around here, but there just isn't time to dwell on it.

Well, there's lots to do and I oughta get at it. I still see our skis and boots standing in the corner of the garage. I can't believe I haven't gotten around to putting them up yet. But if the fireweed's any indication, there's no sense in bothering with it now. I'll be looking for them before you know it, and God knows there's plenty else to do around here.

Halloween

HALLOWEEN is the only holiday I really regret having outgrown. All the other holidays make more sense to an adult (and the food seems better). But there's very little room for a mature and self-controlled individual on Halloween. It's a day of giggles and mischief, tricks and panic sprints in unexplored neighborhoods.

Nine is about the perfect age for Halloween. At nine you're old enough to trick-or-treat without an adult. You can get into a little innocent trouble with a variety of bathroom and dairy products. Yet you're still young enough to look cute in a ghost costume. Later on, during those awkward years between childhood and adolescence, the costumes begin to resemble those of French Resistance fighters. Trick-or-treating is replaced by tactical search-and-destroy missions on unsuspecting pumpkins and school buildings. Of course, that can be fun too, but it's not without its consequences.

I don't remember ever having felt that good about myself after such a mission. There's something evil and definitely unfunny-looking about wet toilet paper dripping off the school shrubbery or wax on the screens the day after Halloween. Not at all the same as the years before. Getting all cranked up on sugar. Trying to eat one more Pixie Stick through the mouth slit in your Spiderman mask as you sneak up to old Mrs. Crabtree's front porch for a treat or a trick. You're all convinced she's a witch, and it takes all the combined courage three nine-year-olds can muster not to bolt down the stairs as the bony old hands open the door. She stares through the storm door menacingly for a few moments, then breaks into a warm and toothless grin as she opens up to offer a full tray of fresh candy apples. You're not going to fall for that old witch trick, so she hands them out, one for each, laughing and lying the whole time that she can't imagine who you all might be. Candy apples were a good score, and you walk away feeling revived and accomplished for having braved the "old witch's" house.

The night goes on. Word would get out on the streets that the Hopkinses were passing out full-sized Baby Ruth bars, and you'd make the special four-block trip just to get one. Later on, when the greasepaint around your mouth would begin to irritate you a little and the purple fake wig was eating a raw spot in your forehead, you'd head home to compare loot with your brothers and sisters. Half-eaten candy apples with fuzz and dirt all stuck to them would be discarded along with any other fruit or produce that may have been collected. Trade and barter would commence with three Smarties buying one Rice Krispie Treat, your Baby Ruth neatly traded for most of your sister's bubble gum.

I miss the days before sugar was bad for you and before moms and dads had to inspect the candy for signs of tampering. Rattling boxes of Red Hots and Good 'n' Plenty building to a brief crescendo as groups of three-and-a-half-foot ghosts and superheros trotted by the streetlights.

I'm probably being just a little oversentimental. But if you should find at your door this Halloween a five-foot ten-inch trick-or-treater with a familiar-sounding voice trying to talk through a pair of those red wax lips with long white fangs, please humor him and give him something. He's just looking for a little of that old-time fun.

Travel Time

ITS THAT TIME of year again. The leaves are history and the familiar whine of studded tires on pavement fills the air. We all knuckle under, pull on the ol' wool coats and hats, sniff the air for signs of snow, and throw a little straw in the dog's house. Signs of winter are everywhere. Backpackers are a rare sight, the travel section in the newspaper gets thicker every week, and house-sitting jobs are easy to come by. Alaskans are taking off like rats from a sinking ship. Normally righteous and hard-working northerners are turning in the oilskins for tacky Polynesian shirts. They're headed off to southern climes to hang around in the sun, frolic in the surf, suck on mangoes, and generally engage in an endless orgy of disgusting and nonproductive behavior. It's a sad sight, and a bit depressing as well, because I can't afford to go with them.

I don't even read the travel section anymore. It puts me in a regular blue funk. Who can read an upbeat account of a Virgin Islands getaway with a clear conscience when he's hoping that his Permanent Fund Dividend check gets here before the electric bill does? I can't. I search around for hurricane stories until I find one that blew down a resort or two. I giggle and gloat over our mild but persistently average weather. It makes me feel better, but it's a false joy.

Those of us who will winter here once again will criticize those that won't. "Fair-weather Alaskans," we'll taunt, "carpetbaggers," take the money and run. We'll pull our fur collars up around our necks and mutter about the pansies that can't take the cold. Well, the heck with all of that. I want to go too.

My wife and I were planning a trip. We looked through the budget and pulled some funds where we could. We saw about cashing in some long-term investments — you know, looked under the bed and behind the couch. We put it all together and decided to take a trip to Kachemak City. We had a wonderful time, but somehow it fell short of the mark.

I'm searching for other means. Maybe we could get somebody to send us somewhere. Like a newspaper or public radio station. They could send us to foreign countries in hopes of getting wry and cynical insights into other cultures. Call it "Insolence Abroad"; I think it could work. I'd take notes and send in weekly installments like, "Boy, there's one thing you can sure say about China: there's an awful lot of Chinese people here." You know, stuff like that. Things the casual observer might miss. I think I'd be good at it, and come springtime we'll all feel a little better traveled.

I'm sending out feelers on this. But if for some reason I can't find an assignment in some warm foreign country, maybe somebody out there can help me find some truck chains to fit a 16 × 7.50 rim. Going to be a long winter by the looks of her.

Christmas Shopping

IF YOU'RE HAVING a hard time getting into the Christmas spirit, try spending a weekend in the big shopping malls. They got the ol' spirit in spades, and they don't mind a bit trying to give you a little. One clerk looked at my wife and me in disbelief. "You mean you haven't entered our Super Christmas Early-Bird Giveaway Sweepstakes? Here, fill these out! We're giving away a ten-pound turkey every fifteen minutes, and a microwave oven on the hour."

Here it is, the day after Thanksgiving, and the last thing on earth that most Americans would like to get is a ten-pound turkey. I got the distinct impression they didn't get rid of quite as many birds as they counted on in their Pre-Thanksgiving Holiday Shopper Special. They've got to make room in the freezers for the Christmas Pack Cheeses and the Yuletide Assorted Santa Snack Candy displays, I guess. That's fair enough.

We filled out our sweepstakes forms but didn't hang around to see any results. Christmas shopping is very serious business. One must move right along in this enterprise if one expects to accomplish anything.

Let's see. Aunt Dolly collects salt and pepper shakers, so we gotta hit a knickknack shop for her. Sister Peg likes sweaters. A football jersey for brother Bob. We always get something brass for my sister-in-law. Good ol' Aunt Marie would just love some of those moose turd doodads — large wild animal feces stuck together with toothpicks to make little toys — quite the gag gift, but where do you find one when you need one? Mom and Dad are too hard to shop for, so maybe we can just throw in with the rest of the family and buy them a barbecue or something.

Then there're the nieces and nephews. My God, toys nowadays are just junk. I couldn't find a toy machine gun to save my life. Everything in the toy stores is from outer space. What kind of a future is there in that? They quit making the Johnny Seven One-Man Army years ago. Now, there was a weapon. It fired single or automatic, had a grenade launcher, a little elastic garrote, a bayonet, and a shoulder harness. That's the kind of all-American toy you can't find anymore. We bought a bunch of flying saucers, tractors, and hand puppets, and we'll sort them out later.

After a while the only names left on our lists were each other's, so we split up and went our separate ways. That's when I realized how exhausted I was. I moseyed into all those fine glass and clock shops to look around. I took a red-faced stroll through a few avant-garde women's clothing stores, and finally ended up on the main thoroughfare.

I found myself staring at some animated elves waving wands at me as a toy train set went round and round in some artificial snow wonderland they'd set up there. I was looking around at some of the other beleaguered shoppers catching a quick five-minute break from Santaland. There among the drawn and solemn faces was the face of my own wife watching that same little plastic elf twirl in circles and bow. We smiled and ended up buying each other a hot pretzel and heading for the car. We'd had enough of the holiday spirit for one weekend.

Christmas shopping can be quite a trial, but what the heck. If it were easy, everybody would be doing it.

Out of Sight,
Out of Season

SCIENTISTS TALK about two different types of existence; matter and antimatter. Well, that's all a lot of hooey. The only two kinds of things in this universe are "things you can't find" and "things that won't go away." Allow me to illustrate.

Everybody owns one of those little three-foot fabric measuring tapes, right? Okay, in five seconds try to remember where yours is at. . . . See what I mean? I'm sure ninety percent of you *thought,* "It's in the junk drawer." No way. That's just where it's *supposed* to be. You didn't know that the kids used it to measure the dog or something last fall, and at this moment it's buried underneath the muck in your front yard. But what *is* in that junk drawer anyway? Probably all your other hard-to-find stuff, you think. Wrong. It's full of the other type of matter, "things that won't go away": the tops to four different ballpoint pens, a can of shoe polish that doesn't match a shoe in the house, two crayons, one dried-up Magic Marker, six dead Bic lighters, and a half-assembled scale model of a World War II antisubmarine bomber. Some stuff.

Junk drawers are the earthly equivalent of limbo. Things that refuse to be refused and just will not go away. Still, we never give up on them. If someone on the phone gives you a number to write down, you go straight for the junk drawer, knowing full well there hasn't been a workable writing implement anywhere near that drawer for the last five years. It's a cosmic phenomenon if I ever heard of one.

How about those tear-out subscription cards that all the magazines are stuffed with? They fall out all over your lap, go behind the couch, and lie in the bottom of the magazine rack. This brings to light a possible third type of matter; "things that won't go away until you need to find them." You can bet that as soon as you decide to subscribe to that magazine, there won't be a coupon in the house. No one really understands the behavior of this third type of matter, so let's stay with what we know about.

Some articles are a lot more willing not to go away than others. Holidays are good for creating this kind of durable matter. Orange-and-white candied corn from Halloween can be found under the refrigerator as late as Christmas, with the needles from your holiday tree churning up in the rug until Easter. Now, the Easter Bunny produces the most mule-headed element yet known to mankind: G.S.E.B.G., Green Synthetic Easter Basket Grass. That stuff is incredible. It will stick to your clothes, adhere to car seats, turn up in your tossed salad, and be brushed out of the dog far beyond the Second Coming itself. I propose to replace the ceramic space shuttle tiles with Easter Basket Grass on the merit of its sheer staying power.

Getting back to "things you can't find," we have some standards: current postage stamps, lids to fit any particular Tupperware container, and all gardening tools with the exception of broken shovels. Broken shovels fall into the classification of "things that won't go away." You've got a handle and you've got a scoop, but you don't have a shovel. Both components are perfectly good with a little modification, but individually worthless until they are remarried. Reconciliations between shovel handles and scoops are so rare in our society as to be negligible, but statistics prove that the separate pieces stay close together, usually in the back of the garage, and they will not go away.

So, as you can see, the makeup of our universe is something other than perfect. It is designed to keep us constantly baffled and mildly frustrated. Philosophers call it "the human predicament." I call it a challenge to be met. My goal is to rid the world of these peculiar and petty nuisances that use up so much of our time and thought. All I have to do is figure out where they are, make them go away, or just figure out how to get along with them.

FAMILY
&
FRIENDS

Grandma Hattie

GOING THROUGH the Christmas cards in our mailbox today, I came across one from my dear old grandma in Illinois. She never fails. Never missed a birthday, Christmas, or anniversary as long as I've lived. Quite a gal, old Grandma Hattie. There's always a nice little letter inside wrapped around a crisp five-dollar bill she can't afford to send.

I read the letter — newsy stuff about her holiday baking and the weather (no snow there yet either). Then as always, there was the postscript at the end: "Just a little Christmas treat. Love, Grandma." So I tucked the five-dollar bill into my shirt and promised that my wife and I would do something extra-special with it. At least as special as five bucks will buy you these days.

Then, as I was reading through the rest of the mail, I came across another card from Grandma. I'll be darned.

Must be our anniversary card, being as we were married the day after Christmas, same as her birthday. She never forgets. I was wrong. It was another Christmas card with another newsy little letter and another brand-new five-dollar bill she couldn't afford to send. Well, what do you think of that?

She must have got confused somehow and forgot to cross us off her list. Or maybe she doesn't have a list. She may do it from memory, and eighty-seven-year-old memories can play tricks like that at times. She may have thought she already sent us one but wasn't altogether sure, so she sent another one just in case. That would be just like her. Rather than take the chance of missing one of us by mistake, she'd send two just to be sure. There aren't many of us that can afford the five dollars that would do that. The heck of it is that I don't dare send it back. She'd be so embarrassed by the mistake, it would do her no good, and I'm sure we can get it back to her in other ways.

There's probably not a whole lot of Christmases left in Grandma Hat, and the world will be the worse for it when she goes. She's endeared herself to friends, family, and strangers alike for many, many decades. My mom tells a story of her from the Depression years.

At the time, Grandma and Grandpa owned a dairy. It was right next door to the house, where the garden is now, and they ran it themselves. They lived near the train tracks, and being that it was during the Depression, they used to get their share of hoboes coming around looking for handouts.

They were hard-working folks, my mom's family, and believed that everybody else should be too. They'd give the "bums," as she called them, food and milk, all right. But

48

they'd have to wash milk cans, scrub floors, shovel snow, or some such thing to get it. Those were the rules, and nobody complained.

Mom says they got pretty popular on the hobo circuit and got that inevitable mark on their front gatepost. Just a little X on the post in white chalk to let the other hoboes know this was a place where a guy could get a handout. It was common practice at that time and was supposed to be on the sly. But Grandma knew it was there. She never did bother any with that chalk on the gatepost, except just once.

It was Christmastime, and my mom was just a little girl. They didn't have any snow yet, but right before Christmas they had a big wind and rain storm. Coming back from church that Sunday, Grandma noticed that the chalk mark had been washed clear off the post by the storm.

It got cold right away like it will on the midwestern plains, and snowed to beat the band. She sat that day in the front room saying the rosary with Grandpa like they always did on Sunday. They saw the hoboes walking down from the train yard going wherever it is hoboes go in a snow-storm. They looked so cold and defeated, but none of them was stopping at the gate or knocking on the dairy window like they always did. Then it struck her why. Of course — the little white X wasn't on the post anymore. Now, where another person might have been relieved to be left alone the Sunday before Christmas, Old Grandma Hat, and she wasn't that old then, put on her overcoat, went right out to the gatepost, and put a great big white X there where nobody could miss it.

I don't know if they got to feed any hoboes that day or not because Mom usually stops telling the story about there, but it doesn't matter. It told me something about Grandma, and I've carried this story with me a long time. She put that X on the gatepost way back then for the same reason she sent us two Christmas cards this year. She didn't want to miss anybody, even if it did cost an extra five bucks. I always think of that story when I'm starting to feel a little broke and put out at Christmastime; then I'm ashamed of myself.

So I don't know what all this means except that in this hard-hearted world we live in, we should all have a gatepost out front, and at least for this one time of year let's all go out and put a great big white X on that thing.

Thirty Candles

IN OUR youth-worshiping society, thirty is supposed to be one of those milestone birthdays when we panic and mistakenly believe that *this* is where we've ended up. Maybe I'm wrong, but I've never felt that way. My age has always had the company of numbers, my having grown up right smack dab in the middle of the baby boom. No matter how old I've been, most everybody I knew was right there with me, and it always seemed pretty normal. Turning the page on thirty seems pretty normal too. Actually, its the best age I've been yet.

At thirty there's just enough years behind us to lend credibility to our ideas, but we've still got our young bodies and the energy to use them. I like it here. No teenage hormones surging around to screw up my judgment, and few naive ideals to clutter my outlook. I wouldn't be eighteen again for love or money. Well, maybe for money.

People who have really racked up the decades are shaking their heads at me right now and thinking what a pup I still am. They're right in a way. Thirty isn't really that old. I could've saved a penny for every day I've lived so far and still not be able to buy a set of snow tires for the car. But at the same time, a lot can happen in thirty years.

Elvis Presley was just entering his heyday when I was born, but I don't think I had anything to do with it. I remember the first television our family bought. It was the size of an industrial clothes drier and had big mahogany doors on it. The first time I saw *Pinocchio* at the movie house they actually played a newsreel. It might have been the last newsreel they ever played, but I saw one. It was about a dog show, and Mamie Eisenhower was there. I saw the Beatles on their first "Ed Sullivan Show" appearance, and we all laughed at their haircuts.

The first and last American soldier to go to Vietnam did so in my time. I was a little too young to go myself, but I had a draft card. Still have half of it here someplace.

I remember the very first *Rolling Stone* magazine and went through a time when I thought Country Joe and the Fish were the only ones who understood me. My first car was a '55 Pontiac Star Chief, and I could still get parts for it. If the radio didn't work, I replaced a tube. Remember tubes?

Yeah, the longer I think about it, the longer I've lived, and the better I like it. Good stuff back there. Good memories. I met the girl who would become my wife when I was fifteen. That's half my life already, and we're going for broke.

No, there's nothing scary about thirty. Our first child will be born in my thirtieth year. A new life assigned to our care for a long time to come. That makes me feel very young.

Some may feel that plans and dreams lose their potency after thirty, but I think they just begin to make sense. Plans turn into deeds, and the dreams are the guidelines. Generations seem to take shape and, God willing, the memories of a good life continue to pile up.

Quite a system we got going here. I cherish the days as they roll by, and can't help but feel that looking backward from sixty can only be twice as nice as it is looking back from here.

Prenatal Paint

I'VE BEEN LEARNING a lot about color lately while my wife and I try to select a color for the new baby's room. I've learned the difference between Fudge Bar and Coco Bar, Flaming Bush and Cherry Bush. You're probably wondering what I'm talking about. It's those names they put on the paint chips. They get me all screwed up. We decided the baby's room should be something bright and cheery, yet nonsexist — you know, like yellow. So I grabbed a bunch of chips down at the paint store. That's where the problem started.

We liked the first one we saw just fine, but then we read the name, Daffodil. I wouldn't have it. What if it's a little boy? I didn't think a daffodil room was in the best interest of his long-term personality development. We'll let him make up his own mind about flowers later on, after football practice. And what about a little girl? It's a little early to be assuming she'll be partial to flowers, isn't it? That choice should be left up to her, maybe after law school. Then there's another one, similar shade, in fact, I can't tell the difference. But the name, Perfect Yellow, come on now. Is anything perfect? We can't have our kid coming to consciousness in a Perfect Yellow room. Any other yellows they might come across for the rest of their days would seem shabby imitations.

"Okay, skip the yellow. How about orange?" I said, pulling out another chip.

"That's not orange, " my wife says, "that's peach."

"No, it's not, says Orange Grove right underneath it."

"I don't care what they call it," she says, "I know peach when I see peach."

"Well, that might be, dear, but the color right below it is Cantaloupe. Now, what's it going to be?" We had to take a break at this point to get something to eat.

Feeling refreshed, we tackled a different color: green. Now, green is a strange one. To me it only looks good on trees. On anything else it looks cheap and depressing. But you wouldn't know it by the names they give it: Gypsy Queen, South Pacific, Jubilee Green. I think they're trying to make up with semantics for what these shades lack in appeal. You can call it South Pacific all day long, but it's still going to be green that night.

Okay, never mind the greens, let's take a look at lavenders. My wife was surprised I even knew what color lavender was, but I was more surprised to find that they have at least a dozen different shades of it. They say the Eskimos have eight different names for snow. These guys have got twelve different names for purple. Grape Accent, that one makes sense. Azalea, I'll have to take their word on that.

Then there's one called Chris. Who's Chris? Or Capricious. I guess you don't know what that color will do once you get it on the wall. They have a whole chip just for social climbers: High Society, Front Royal, Bishop's Purple. There, they said it, purple. I knew it. I hate purple.

We weren't getting anywhere and were both beginning to feel a little blue. Not Party Blue, or Patch-of-Blue, but a regular Royal-Glow-Blue.

"Let's just paint it off-white like the rest of the house," my wife said.

"Sounds fine with me. What do you like here? Decorator White? Rice Paper? How about Bamboo Orchid with Alabaster Highlight? Or maybe this Wheatstraw?"

She snapped about then and left it up to me. She doesn't care what they call it, just as long as it's off-white. So I'm looking for a can of paint that says "Off-White." There has to be one out there someplace. I'm also looking for a book of baby's names that has only two names in it, a boy's and a girl's. We're going to talk about that next weekend.

Baby Names

I THINK I'd rather take a beating than look at another book of baby names. We have one book here with seven thousand names in it and another with four thousand, and we don't like any of them. Oh, it's not that we don't like any of them, we just can't pick one. How can we name something we've never even seen? How can we put a stranger's name on our child? We need some help. What ever happened to the rules?

Some families have guidelines that go back centuries. The first son is named after the first son of the paternal grandparent with the mother's maiden name as the middle name — that sort of thing. Some religions suggest we name all the children after saints, but that's outdated, and besides it didn't narrow the field all that much to begin with.

Most of the common names have been used up by the baby boom; lotta Toms, Dicks, and Harrys running around.

So we swing the other way and try to come up with unique names that stand out a little. Now, unique names that stand out a little are real common too. The Jeremiahs and Jessicas of today are the Johns and Marys of tomorrow.

We go through trends, like when everybody had to name their dogs after Tolkien characters — Strider, Frodo, Gandolph; one in every pickup truck. Dogs are easy to name, though, because they don't care what their names are as long as you call them something. But a kid will grow up to hate you as only a kid can if you give him a rotten name. You gotta watch out for names that cruel little playground kids can turn into insults. The hell of it is that mean little kids can turn almost any name into an insult if they've a mind to. Sooner or later the child's going to come home crying no matter what you call them. So I'm just stumped.

I was trying to think up just a normal boy's name when I thought, "Why not just name him Normal?" Good ol' Norm. Guaranteed a life of listless mediocrity. No matter what he grew up to do or become, he would always be Normal. The sheer poetry of it had me excited, but my wife stepped in and put an end to the thought. It must be remembered that mothers have ultimate veto power in the naming process.

We've got lots of time yet, but there're no solutions in sight. I'm all for waiting until we meet the little beggar, then decide what or who they remind us of. Or do like the Indians and name them after a natural phenomenon or significant occurrence observed during pregnancy or on the day of the birth. It would surely be unique and personal. It might date them and offer a sense of place and heritage. Like Datsun-that-won't-start-when-its-cold or Slick-spot-on Bartlett-Street. That would be on the birth record, but we

could call them Dotty or Bart. The prospect excites me —
the chance to document through nomenclature important
historical events. Like if the Seahawks went to the Super
Bowl, stuff like that. I guess I'll just have to wait and see
what happens.

I picture myself fifteen years from now sitting down
with the grown child to explain the significance of their
name to them. They'll look up into my proud face and say:
"You know, Dad? You're a real jerk."

Mother's
Many Helpers

HAVING SPENT the last sev-
en months living with a pregnant woman, I've come to the
conclusion that there're worse things in this world than
being pregnant, but I can't for the life of me think of what
they might be. If there's an ailment, symptom of an ailment,
or inconvenience that the human form can acquire, a pregnant woman will get it sometime during her term. If she's
sick all the time and can't eat, the doctor will tell her,
"Nothing to worry about. It's all part of being pregnant."
Then, later on, when she's hungry all the time and all she
does is eat, that's part of it too. Sleep too much? Comes
with the program. Can't sleep at all? That's to be expected.
Vanishing navels, undue toe jam, or rickets — apparently
nothing is a surprise to find happening to a pregnant
woman. My heart goes out to her, and all mothers every-

where. Not only do they have to tolerate all of these minor and major medical inconsistencies, but they must also put up with a thick and steady stream of unsolicited advice and sympathies.

It seems people perceive expectant mothers as a hands-on experience. It's not uncommon for a relative stranger to walk up to one, pat her on her protruding belly, and offer up a few words of congratulations, or worse. People wouldn't dare reach into her coat and touch her front under normal circumstances, but the fact that she's pregnant makes her into a sort of human Blarney Stone. One touch of the blessed bulge and the tongues start wagging. "How far along are you? Oh, really, you just wait. The worst is yet to come." Or, "You've *got* to get yourself a wind-up swing, they are the greatest thing since disposable diapers. Speaking of which, go for the Huggies, they're the best. Luvs are good, but, oh boy, are they spendy." And on and on until pretty soon you've got a group of women standing around comparing stretch marks and hip profiles. Not having been endowed with the functions of motherhood, this can all seem quite strange to a mere mortal like myself.

Parenthood is an endless list of truisms and folk tales that nobody ever gets tired of repeating. From morning sickness to the "terrible twos," everything is made out to sound exactly seven times as bad as it really is. It seems to me these poor women have enough on their minds without all that bad news to boot.

If you were to give me an extra twenty-five pounds to pack around all crammed against my more delicate seams and organs, stirred my hormones around some for effect, and then walked up and started in on some smug speech about how bad it was going to get later on, I think I'd break your nose for you. It's probably all for the best that people like me don't get pregnant.

It takes a special kind of person to get through pregnancy gracefully. Any old dumbbell can get pregnant and have kids; they've been doing it for thousands of years. But it takes an even more special woman to have a baby and not pester others with a lot of unwanted advice.

My hat's off to all mothers wherever they might be. Let's give them a little breathing room.

Birth Rites

Watching OUR CHILD being born held a moment of joy, mixed, I think, with just a little bit of terror. He came out swinging and squirrely. He looked around with my eyes and curled up a mouth that was clearly his mother's.

A feeling of utter incompetence swept over me as he launched into his first scream of this world. I mean, this little guy is a pretty fancy piece of equipment, but it didn't come with any instructions. Sure, there's a library full of books on child care, but they're all "schools of thought." All they can seem to agree on is that infants on the whole are very young and they will change your life. They appeared, for the moment, to be right on both counts, but that didn't offer us much support just then.

Pains of inadequacy soon gave way to genuine concern, and I began the classic drill of counting fingers and toes. Everything checked out and most of my fears subsided, the exception being his tendency to cross his eyes back and forth like a fish.

Immediate concerns melded easily into long-range apprehension of this poor baby's future injuries and the heartbreaks bound to come his way. With clear pangs of guilt I imagined myself reluctantly and maybe unjustly punishing him in years to come. I felt myself bracing for confrontations that he would not be able to engineer for at least a decade.

The mere thought of this little baby one day conspiring against us flashed me to anger. I pictured him speeding off on some futuristic two-wheeled death trap. He had a metallic hairdo and "Born to Raise Goats" or some equally awful slogan printed on the back of his titanium road jacket. I cursed all powers who made it so that generations must irritate each other in order to change things and forge ahead in this world.

My mind raced with adrenaline aided by six hours' worth of hospital coffee. As I grabbed a breath and took in the scene in front of me, it struck me how entirely insignificant all my worrying — and me as the father, period — really were at that moment.

My wife lay there smiling after completing several hours of the hardest work I'd ever seen anyone, man or woman, do. With their flesh-and-blood connection freshly severed by my hand, the baby took to his mother with that sort of primordial ease that can only be described as a miracle whatever your religious bent, or lack of, might be. As she lay there with her son, exhausted and in an unflattering position, I could only think that I'd never seen her quite so beautiful.

Our child soon went to sleep, contented, and agreed to his new status in life. My wife, as well, drifted off to euphoric rest. I drifted back toward the coffee pot trying to capture the moment.

All I was able to nail down for sure was what a wonder it all is, and how much old Mother Nature really does require of her daughters.

ISSUES
&
OBSERVATIONS

The Group That
Notices Things

THERE IS a group of anony-
mous people running around who I think deserve some
recognition. They are seldom pretentious and almost always nondiscriminatory. They are the GNTs, the Group
That Notices Things. You might know one. You might even
be one. They wear no insignia, but the look in their eye is
a dead giveaway. Its like they have their brights on most of
the time.

There was one in front of me on the way to town one
day who was nursing an old Ford Fairlane down the highway. I was in my typical morning panic, waiting impa-
tiently for a straightaway to pass her on. Well, this particular GNT noticed my predicament, sensed the frenzy, and
pulled over at the first available wide spot to let me go on
my way. That one was easy to spot. Almost everyone who

uses their rearview mirror belongs to the Group That Notices Things.

I saw this dump-truck driver. He was pulled over to the side of the road and up on top of his load kicking rocks and gravel in from the edges. He must have noticed he was dribbling stones from on top of the pile brimming over the truck and decided he'd waste five minutes of his precious day rather than take the chance of putting out somebody's windshield. Definitely a member in good standing of the GNTs.

Then there's this lady down at the store. She's got a cart and a half of groceries, two kids, and what looks like an awful bad attitude. Then all of a sudden she turns around and sees me standing there with a pack of Beechnut in my hand and my normal expression of manic acceleration on my face. She says, "Oh, you go ahead, I'm in no hurry." Can you believe that? For that busy lady to notice me and let me go on by her just because I was only buying a pack of chewing tobacco that'll give me ulcers someday anyway, now that's a heck of a gesture. She was without a doubt a card-carrying member of the Group That Notices Things. All hats off, please, to this fine human being.

By now you're wondering how to get into this elite corps of perceptive and well-mannered people. It's as easy as using your turn signal at Pioneer and Ocean Drive. All you gotta do is notice what's going on around you and see if there isn't some simple little thing you can do to make it go on a little easier. Do that for a week solid and you're a member, no questions asked. Very few are turned away.

Those that do things like let their kids swing on those red felt ropes at movie theaters so they knock the little brass stands over will have a tough time qualifying, as will those that still think El Salvador is an imported Mexican beer. Hacky Sack players, though not ineligible, are rigorously screened only because the Group That Notices Things hasn't noticed anything at all particularly interesting about that game. Outside of that, the GNTs maintain a fairly open roster.

Take a look around and give it a try. Join the group that is dedicated to the long life of perception in general and the defeat of mindless activity in particular. Turn on your brights and put it in gear. Don't worry about making a spectacle of yourself in front of friends and family. Nobody outside the Group is going to notice it anyway.

Reasonable
Doubts

I T'S HARD for me to get irritated by the issues. I guess I just don't have a political mind. By the time something bothers me enough where I get worried about it, somebody's already taken care of it and there's nothing to get mad about anymore. It's like cleaning house. My wife cleans it, not because I wouldn't, but she never lets it get dirty enough for me to worry about.

I felt bad about this and thought I should try to get riled about something, so I looked through the paper for some infraction of justice, flagrant discrimination, and rampant skullduggery in general. There's lots to choose from, but picking sides on complex issues can be quite a chore. There's this fur seal hunt on the Pribilof Islands. Seems these seals might be getting hard to come by before long, so they'd like to stop this hunt. Well, hell, I thought,

I might like to see a fur seal if I'm ever out that way, so it looked like a good thing to get mad about. As I looked into it, though, I found out that it's not just the hunt that's got everybody upset, but that they hunt 'em with clubs and beat 'em to death. Well, shoot, I guess that'd make about anybody mad, beatin' up seals, so I started to get a little worked up. Well, the more I read into it, the stickier it got. Seems if the natives don't hunt these seals, it invalidates some international trade agreement, and any ol' foreigners could come in and harvest 'em any way they please. Death rays, probably. Well, it seemed like the natives needed the seals to live on, and there aren't a whole lot of natives left either, and the whole thing was getting so confusing I decided I better look around for something else to get mad about.

Then there's this outfit that wants to capture our killer whales and put them in an aquarium in Ohio or someplace. Wouldn't that get ya going? Take an intelligent critter like that and put him in a fish tank so kids with ice cream on their faces can gawk and shriek at him. I say leave 'em here so we can gawk and shriek at them. There may even be a shortage of them, probably is, but I wouldn't know, livin' up in the hills like I do. So just as I was starting to get good and mad about catching orca whales, I read that they live a hundred years and eat fur seals the whole time. Well, we're trying to save those too, and I couldn't pick a favorite out of the two, so I backed down on both counts and dug around some more.

There in the lower right-hand corner of the editorials was a question: "What should Anchorage do about the Pitbulls?" God, I'd found it. Something I could be offended by. It seems the Anchorage health officials are preventing the

73

adoption of pitbulls from their dog pound because they've proven themselves to be a public menace. Dog owners are up in arms about it. It's discrimination, they say, animal racism. You bet it is. Now they got me going. Who's to say that any old dog, my black Lab maybe, couldn't commit just as many heinous crimes as those wimpy dogs? I aim to prove that my black Lab is capable of being a dangerous criminal, and then I'll show he's discriminated against because he is one. After that I'll see if I can get him a state job through an affirmative-action program and start a college fund for my kids with his wages.

Maybe they'll grow up smart enough to care about what matters and only get upset over the really important things.

Elections

WOULDN'T IT be fun to watch a second-grade class act out an American election? They could divide into groups and nominate candidates to voice their concerns to their teacher, Miss Norton. I can just hear the debates that might take place.

As one crew-cut lad stands, he says, "If elected, I will represent *every* member of the second-grade class. Boys and girls alike. I want to dispel once and for all this notion that girls have cooties."

There are cheers from the girls as many of them run from the opponent's corner to join him.

"Hold on just a minute," hollers the opponent. "This second-grade class is at a pivotal point in the school year. We need strong leadership that can effectively make our needs clear to Miss Norton. You want leaders like me and my vice, Charlie." Charlie opens his Star Wars lunch box and tosses out Life Savers and Scoobie-do lick-'em tattoos to the gathered crowd. "And furthermore," he squeaks, holding up his hands, "I have it from a reliable source, namely my opponent's kid sister Rita, that he still sucks his thumb at night! Is this the kind of leadership we want in this classroom?"

"No!" screams the sugar-crazed crowd, mimicking thumb-sucking to the cowering boy in the opposite corner.

Regaining his composure, the stung kid defiantly exclaims, "I wanted to leave this sort of mudslinging out of the campaign, but I see how easily my opponent forgets the time he wet in his snow pants down at the sled hill, then sat in my mom's car without telling anyone. You can still see the stain on the seat!"

He stands back triumphantly as hoots and hollers erupt from voters running wildly about the classroom feigning bladder pains and jumping on one foot. The campaign drones on from one disgusting exposé to the next until Miss Norton finally gives up and forces a vote.

Yes, it would be interesting to see children imitating an adult political campaign. Almost as interesting as it is watching the adult campaigners imitate children. The issues are a little different, very little in some cases, but it all ends up the same.

Our own Miss Norton forces our vote too, and it's we who must decide many times, and in many different races, between the kid who sucks his thumb, and the one who wet his pants.

Here's to hoping those kinds of things don't mean as much to us as they would like to think, and that we've got a little better sense and good taste than Miss Norton's class does.

I'm not sure we do, but here's hoping anyway.

The
Tourist Trade

I'D LIKE to say something about tourists. I think we're way too hard on them here in Homer. We go to our favorite vacation spots like Hawaii and get called things like *haole,* which just means "white person," or in Mexico it's *gringo,* which is "outsider" or "newcomer," near as I can figure out. Maybe in the South we'll get called a Yankee, which carries no malice in it other than meaning you're not from Dixie.

But what do we call all of them when they come here? Pukers. Come on now, *pukers?* Give 'em a break. It's not like they move around town throwing up on things, at least not many of them. A few of them do earn the moniker out on the charter boats, but there's just a handful of unfortunate deckhands that have to worry about that. All in all they really haven't done too much to deserve it.

On the whole they're a pretty harmless and amiable bunch. Sure, they drive too slow and wear dumb clothes, but imagine if everybody in Homer invited all their relatives up the same summer. The scene would look about as it does every summer. These are just the folks back home come to see us. We should treat them like they were our roommate's parents.

They don't seem to bother us all that much. Most of them *drive* to town, which means they've probably asked all the really dumb questions somewhere up the road. We don't have to answer a lot of "Is that snow?" questions, or have too many people ask to see a picture of our Queen. The border and fringe towns have to put up with that sort of thing.

By the time they get here, they're just wondering how the fish are biting and if the milk is fresh. Although I admit to having one ask me what the elevation of Homer was as we looked out over the ocean; anybody could get their latitudes and altitudes turned around. He could've been from Kansas, or even Indiana. Give him a break.

Just remember when you were in Hawaii with your skin scorched bright red and a great big blob of white sunscreen on your beak, and be grateful the natives didn't make a big deal out of it. There is nothing on this earth as grotesque as an Alaskan's first day on the beach, and here we sit in judgment of people who wear checkered pants with captain's hats. God, at least they have clothes on.

At any rate, I kinda get a kick out of them. Feels nice that these folks would come all that way to see where I live. Makes me appreciate it a little more myself, and remember why I first came here and asked a lot of dumb questions.

Private Pains

THE DAMNDEST THING happened while I was driving down Pioneer Avenue last week. I was passing an intersection and noticed a middle-aged lady stopped in her car waiting to enter the road. There was nothing remarkable about the car, but I happened to look at just the right time and saw she was crying.

Her cheeks were wet and her mouth was sort of twisted in that sorrowful half-smile people sometimes get when they cry. She didn't seem to be in any kind of predicament, and I'd never seen her before, so I did what we usually do when we see people crying; I looked away and drove on.

I kept thinking about it as I drove down the road. What could have driven this woman to tears in the middle of the day while waiting at a stop sign? Maybe she'd just gotten some terrible news about something. Maybe a parent had died or her husband left her. Perhaps a child was hurt at school and she was panicked and on her way there at that very moment. It could have been her birthday or anniversary, and her family had gone off to work and school without saying anything about it. Who could tell?

It might even have been something rather silly. She may have been coming from her hairdresser, who'd done an absolutely horrible job on her, and she didn't know how she'd face people. Or found that she'd inadvertently *not* been invited to her club luncheon that day. Maybe she was just having one of those days we all have from time to time, and trying to make a left turn onto Pioneer Avenue in lunch-hour traffic was the last straw this poor woman could bear.

I wanted to turn around and go ask her what was wrong, but I knew she'd be gone by then. Even if she wasn't, I didn't think she'd talk to a stranger about it. I had a brief vision of opening her car door and holding her, telling her it would be all right. But I knew I would never do that, and would probably get arrested if I did.

It bugged the heck outa me. Wondering what kind of tragedy this woman was carrying with her and enduring by herself. I thought about the sadness we all carry with us every day, and take to bed with us at night. The small pains and disappointments that keep us off our mark a little. They make us snap at store clerks without meaning to, or beep our horns at a slowpoke even when we're in no particular hurry. The sadness that sits like a chip on our shoulders, daring anyone to touch it. It makes our mouths taut and our eyes steely. We move stiffly, looking at our feet when we walk, lost in our own little worlds.

This woman, all alone in her car and for no apparent reason, had let her taut mouth fold and her steely eyes fill with tears. The tears came easier with every car that rolled by and left her there, myself included.

Possibly she was the store clerk someone had snapped at, or the slowpoke that got honked at. I don't know, I'm just guessing. It seems we spend so much time torturing each other to get to the head of the line or maneuver into that last parking space. Maybe we should forget about all that stuff every once in a while and just keep our eyes peeled for the tears of a stranger.

Contraries

IT DOESN'T MATTER what it is or where you are. Whatever it is the powers-that-be decide to do about something, there's somebody there that doesn't like it. That's to be expected, but what gets me is that it's always the same people who don't like it. Every time. Don't these people have jobs?

I think it was Shaw, maybe it was Mark Twain, coined a word for these folks. They're called contraries. Now, I think that what that means is that none of these people are happy unless something is going wrong. Either that, or if you're for it, they're against it. Must be a hobby, like debate club.

They look at themselves as the watchdogs of government and industry, but it's like having a dog that barks all the time. Pretty soon you don't pay any attention to it, and when you do, it does little more than irritate the hell out of you. You'd think they'd move around a little. Rotate the serve like a volleyball team. Maybe even come out in favor of something every so often just to catch us off guard. Put Ralph Nader in a Chrysler commercial. Wake us up a bit.

I look at bureaucracy like it is a cockroach. Now, the cockroach is extremely adaptable to a wide range of abuses. Keep spraying the same ol' bug spray at a cockroach and pretty soon it doesn't bother him anymore. Maybe even gets him a little high. Well, it doesn't seem to bother governments and conglomerates to have the same guys up there raggin' at 'em week after week either. After a while they become immune to it. So what I think these contraries should do is get together and freshen the field a bit.

They could form an association. No particular platform or philosophy would be necessary, just an underlying desire to mix it up a little. Adversaries Anonymous. Must be a lot of closet complainers out there who are just chompin' the bit but have no particular cause to harass. They could have meetings and delegate responsibilities and assignments.

"Joe, you write the congressmen. They want to change the colors of the license plates this year, and I want to know why. Ask them if they have a chemical breakdown of the new color scheme. I don't like to sound of that red stuff.

"Amy, you get one off to the highway department. I've been seeing far too many rabbit casualties along the road lately, and I want to see what they're doing about it. Ask about rabbit crosswalks, maybe. Send a copy to Greenpeace; we may need help on this one.

"Wilbur, I think it's your turn at the City Council meeting this week. Just pick something off the agenda and run with it. You know what to do.

"And everybody, please remember the Group Gripe this Thursday. Bring a guest and be on time. I hate it when you're late. Bring those petitions and let's get 'em signed, whatever they're for."

The Big City

M Y WIFE AND I have always considered ourselves reasonably worldly and well-adjusted people. We drive defensively, shop wisely, brush regularly, and don't take candy from strangers. In spite of our self-image, however, there's nothing like spending a weekend in the big city to make you feel like a hayseed. You can take the hick out of the small town, but you can't take the small town out of the hick; in fact, you can't take them hardly anyplace.

Anchorage isn't that big of a place as far as cities go, but it's all we've got, and quite big enough to make a fool out of most of us small-towners.

It all starts, of course, in the shopping centers, shopping being the only logical reason to endeavor to the city in the first place. The huge chain stores are chock-full of merchandise that I just vaguely remember having existed;

so, understandably, we needed one of each. The list of items we really came for is lost in a fit of feverish consumerism: from ten-pound boxes of generic talcum powder to cheap beveled mirrors in fake oak frames. Our shopping carts begin to resemble the supply line for Lewis and Clark's First Expeditionary Force.

Then you run into all the unfamiliar big-store rules.

"I'm sorry, sir, we can't sell you that lamp. It's our display model and we have no more in stock."

"Oh, I don't mind," we say. "I'll pay full price for it. We really like that one."

"Sir, if we sell you that one, we won't have a display model."

"Well, if you sell me the last one, you won't need a display model, will you?"

"You'll have to speak with our management about that."

"Okay, where are they?"

"Houston."

We walk away perplexed and convinced that large department stores are the training fields for our future government bureaucrats.

Having survived the shopping excursion, we lumber away in a compact car loaded to the napes of our necks and search around for a place to eat. Several months of unrelieved commercial television indoctrination lead us inevitably to a fast-food joint of one disgusting sort or another. We order all kinds of burgers with trick names accompanied by unlikely-looking french fries, and feel somewhat foolish for taking that same old bait yet again.

Vowing never to eat at another place that advertises on TV or admits to being "family dining," we quest ever onward in search of distraction. After blundering through an endless string of illegal left turns and random lane changes, we spy a quite unexpected surprise. Gas for less than a buck a gallon, and a free car wash to boot. Our mouths agape in wonder, we pull in to top off the tank and rinse several miles of dirt road surfacing off the car.

Cueing up to the entrance of the automatic car wash, we confessed to one another that neither had been through a totally automated wash before. A grim-looking attendant came out without a word, unscrewed the antenna, plucked the wiper blades, and tossed them through the window at my wife, who was driving. Not being aware of proper car wash protocol, we drove forward with the window still down to inquire as to what our next move should be. This was extremely well timed, with the first shot of high-pressure prewash nearly drowning us both. We peered through the haze to see the attendant holding up a large sign with black lettering informing us to "Keep all windows closed. Put car in neutral. Don't step on brakes!" "Sounds easy enough," we said, sitting back to towel ourselves off.

The machine dragged us through a dark gauntlet of suds, rollers, and whirling barrages of what looked like kelp slapping against the windshield. It spat us out the other end in due course, where the bemused attendant put our antenna back and replaced the wipers. Feeling a bit flustered, we pulled out into the one-way street to escape the workman's pitiful smirk.

We looked up just in time to see five full lanes of traffic heading our way at high speed. Experiencing what the German sentries at Normandy Beach must have felt when the Allied invasion fleet crested the horizon, we made a hasty U-turn, which took us once more past the car wash. The attendant, having witnessed the whole scene, just looked at me and shook his head. It was then that I realized that with my wife doing the driving, he must have figured she was the smart one, so I hid my face in my hamburger wrapper.

We were at about the end of our rope.

"Hey," I said. "Whatcha say we drive all night in a snowstorm and go home?"

"Sounds good to me," she said, accelerating out of town. After all, driving in white-out conditions at two in the morning through a desolate mountain pass sipping cold coffee from a Stanley steel thermos, is something we can understand.

PART 5

THE
WORKING
LIFE

Winter Construction

IF YOU'RE LYING around the house this winter bored and in search of new distractions, I've got a real winner here. "Winter Construction." It's an attractive sport to the athletic-minded, as it utilizes skill, concentration, and dexterity, and is more fun than falling off a house.

Allow me to point out a few of its finer features.

First, the uniform. Start with a pair of insulated boots that must weigh at least nine pounds apiece. Then add a cotton/wool union suit, canvas pants, heavy flannel shirt, a Thinsulate padded jacket, and an insulated rugged-duty cotton coverall over the whole works. To fall within the legal guidelines of this sport you should now scale in at about half again your normal weight and look roughly like a Cabbage Patch doll in a brown paper sack.

Newcomers to the sport will experience some of the early pitfalls but soon learn that nails freeze to your lips at about twenty degrees. So just keep them in your hand. The pain of smashing your own thumb with a hammer is multiplied by one hundred times for every ten degrees below freezing and has been known to bring tears to the eyes of even the most seasoned participants. Smashing one's own extremities at these colder temperatures has been known to cause fainting in some frailer souls and should be avoided at all costs. Remember also that nylon gloves melt on contact with kerosene space heaters, and the crew boss is sure to keep the anxiety levels high by reiterating to you time and again how fast he did the same job back in July.

The game begins early in the morning and is exhilarating from the start. The first task is to pull the coverings from the lumber piles and beat the fight out of them with an eight-pound maul. This frees the boards from one another. Now, there is nothing in this world quite as slippery as two layers of plastic with snow in between. You can fall on your duff at velocities approaching the speed of light and catch that eight-pounder in what is guaranteed to be an unfortunate location.

Then the real fun begins.

You waddle up to an aluminum ladder perched precariously on a patch of ice and climb up two stories in a uniform which does not allow you to bend your knees. Once there, you find that you can effectively split a twelve-foot roof rafter with one ten-penny nail. Here's where you employ some tricks of the trade. To keep the wood from splitting, some spit on their nails. Some people lay a cross pattern on the board at the point of nailing. And still others look to the morning star and make a wish for the best.

Myself, I prefer to ignore the whole situation and head directly for the saw. Before you can make a cut, you must, of course, mark your board. In summer a pencil or crayon is commonly used, but in Winter Construction a large nail or sharp chisel is a much more intelligent choice. Just scratch the ice and saw away. It's as easy as that. The entire operation is done with large leather fleece-lined gloves and provides a challenge equivalent to playing tennis with galvanized steel buckets on your feet.

So come on out and join the fun. We start at eight sharp, and of course there is no wage. We wouldn't want to compromise anyone's amateur status.

Researchers

I'VE DECIDED that I want to be a researcher. It sure sounds easy. I hear on the news that research has determined that animals like to be stroked and patted. Who'da thought? I picture a lot of grim technicians in white smocks standing around a dog thumping its hind leg on the floor as it gets its belly scratched. They take notes, and fifty thousand dollars' worth of government research grants later, they announce to us that "Yes, folks, your pets do like to be petted." Thank God. I thought my cat might have just been faking it for me.

Then there's this other one they just came out with. "Grief and worry can lead to a premature death." That's pretty serious stuff, but I can remember my mother scolding many years ago, "Now, Mrs. Bibbs is a lonely old lady and she likes you kids, so be nice to her." We were nice to her, still are whenever we get home. That's right. She's still alive. My mother diagnosed this ailment twenty years before the researchers came up with it, and also prescribed a cure that worked. Now, had she been a psychologist with a knack for writing grant proposals, she might have made a little money and got her picture in the paper. Unfortunately, all she had was common sense and a warm heart, and her only reward has been having a kindly old widow lady for a neighbor for twenty years or so. I guess Mom missed her calling. She should have been a researcher.

I've been studying it, and I think I've got the hang of this research business. Just pick something, and prove it. Here's a couple I'm trying to get money for at the moment. "If you back up a car without looking, you'll run into something." Laugh if you will, but it's not easy to prove. It's going to take quite a bit of government subsidy to conduct this study.

One person will jump in the car, back up, and smack into something right off the bat. So you mark that down. Then the next one does the same thing. You mark that down. Then you get some lucky buck who can back up blind from here to Wednesday and never hit a thing. It throws the average off, so you have to get five more direct hits to prove your point. You can see how this research business could get expensive.

Research isn't always just determining *what* happens. Sometimes they even find out *why.* That's the objective of my other study. "Why does everyone who calls in to those radio sell-'n'-swap programs sound like my aunt Marie from Arkansas?" I don't see anything wrong with it; I just want to know why. Could be anything. Maybe it *is* my aunt, doing it just to bug me because I never go visit her. Maybe they're just friends of hers. Perhaps there's some kind of audio modulation that occurs in the transition from phone line to radio wave that causes it. Maybe all those people really talk that way. No one knows right now.

It's questions like these that keep the research business alive, and we aim to answer them. There's a reason for everything even if you don't care what it is.

Dress
for Success

A WHILE BACK I was read-
ing about this business seminar they had. "Dress for Success" they called it. Kind of a traveling self-improvement
deal. Wish I'd have went, in a way. Anybody that can get
people to pay them for that sort of thing is worth getting
a look at. It might have done me some good too, but I
doubt it. Everything is too calculated these days. Dressing
seems like a personal choice like "What do you want for
supper?" It's not something that can be taught at a seminar.
Seems like everybody would come out of there looking all
the same. Why don't they just join the military and have
done with it?

What kind of success are they talking about anyway?
Around here successful dressing means you're staying
warm and dry. Every situation has got its own little wardrobe requirements. If I went into the hardware store

dressed like I was at my wedding, they'd think I was a tool salesman and I'd never get waited on. At the same time, if I went to the bank in the clothes I do my writing in, they'd throw me out. The only reason it looks silly is that the propeller on my beanie is broke and the black cape and mask clash with my rabbit slippers.

We find ourselves in so many different kinds of situations; how can we possibly dress effectively to meet them all? That's why I try to hang around in the neutral zone between bad taste and no taste whatsoever.

It's pretty easy to get my half of the dresser confused with the rag drawer. There's some nice clothes in there too, but I don't wear them. I'm one of those "favorite shirt" kind of guys. My favorite shirt was a pretty nice flannel job once upon a time, a Big Mack. Anyone who's ever had a favorite shirt will know what I'm talking about. It's not that I feel good or sharp in that shirt; I just feel *right* in it. It's part of me, like my hands are. So just like my hands, I wore it about every day for as long as I can remember; but unlike my hands, I wore it out. At least my wife says I did. I never noticed.

So my good ol' favorite shirt has disappeared from my half of the closet and been replaced by a short stack of new shirts. Big deal. They look like somebody else's shirts. I just can't warm up to them. Favorite clothes are born of apathy. You don't notice them. That's why you end up wearing them all the time.

But there's no getting around these new shirts. Two green ones and a red one. Very Christmasy. This gives a clue to their origins and explains why I had no say in picking them out. Now I take off my coat in restaurants and all the eyes in the room sort of drift over to me. I'd rather wear clothes that made people look away, if anything. That's probably why I've been gravitating toward radio work. Nobody really cares what you wear on the radio. At least not so far. Though sometimes it is hard to keep the chiffon from rustling in the microphone.

I have no head for fashion. I never upgrade my wardrobe; I replace it, and then only under duress. You don't find me thumbing through the double-knits or holding up pastel-colored pullovers with reptiles on the pockets. Those are other people's clothes.

I've dressed the same way since high school. People I haven't seen in ten years will shake my hand and say, "By God, Tom, you look just the same." Well, of course I do, it's the same shirt. I like that. I think it keeps me looking young, but my wife thinks it keeps me looking like the janitor at the J. C. Penney store. What the heck, so we have the same tailor. I'm comfortable, he's comfortable, and in my way of thinking, comfort *is* success.

Just keep your fly zipped, don't button your top button, and you'll probably do just fine.

Beard
Ranching

THEY GOT something for everybody nowadays. Seminars for the ill-dressed, therapy groups for the ill at ease, clinics for the drugged and drinking, and fat farms for the obese. But there's one social problem that I find no one addressing: growing a new beard. How about a Beard Ranch? A place where a guy struggling with his novice whiskers can do so in peace. It would provide an ideal atmosphere with no mirrors and the constant companionship of sheepish men with patchy faces and no sideburns. House rules would prohibit the mention of facial hair in any way. Patrons would spend a lot of time roping calves, chopping wood, and working on heavy machinery. This would get the macho-male glandular system stimulated to promote hair growth.

I'd be their first customer.

Growing a new beard in the public eye can be an awkward and humiliating experience. The first few days aren't so bad. It looks like you forgot to shave, or just got back from a fishing and hunting trip. After that things begin to fall apart, at least for me.

My stubble will grow like a weed until it reaches the point where I'm a dead ringer for a criminal drifter with an affinity for fruit-flavored carbonated wines, and then it sort of stalls out there. God only knows for how long. I've tried to get through this dormant stage before, but something always interfered; like I had to get married, open a checking account, do jury duty, or some such thing that required me to shave. So this time I'm going to try to tough it out. I'm old enough that my manhood's not in question, and sometimes it's to one's advantage to look like a criminal drifter. Like when insurance salesmen call, or you find yourself sitting next to a real-estate agent down at the coffee shop.

In spite of these slim assets, cultivating a passable Vandyke or even a pencil-thin mustache can be a painful chore. My friends are mostly friend enough not to mention it, but other folks can be quite cruel. "Gettin' a little fuzz on the peach, eh, boy?" they'll say, or, "Whatcha do, lose your razor, or do you just try to wash that stuff off?" Real cute. The only thing worse is when you see people that *do* notice it but divert their eyes and pretend like they didn't. I get uncomfortable and lose my train of thought, say something inadequate, and walk away scratching my chin just like it itches.

Getting the ol' premiere bristle into focus is not something a fella should have to endure unassisted. I think I'll start that Beard Ranch myself. Heck of an idea. I'm sure there's thousands of rag-faced warriors out there that would pay handsomely for the service. I can compile a feasibility study of the project and scout out some suitable remote location for the thing.

I'll take it all down to the banks and try to win them over for financial backing. Of course, I better shave this garbage off my chin first. I can't go anywhere looking like this.

The
Slow Life

To SAY THAT life in Alaska is slow would be an understatement. I come from the Midwest, where things are in second gear at best, and have lived in Alaska so long I've dropped right down into granny. There's people here will take half an hour just to think of something to say. I've left conversations dangling for better than a week, and found the next time I run into the guy, neither one of us has even lost his train of thought. Must be too much oxygen in the air around here or something.

Only time we move fast is when the front door blows open. How could you be in a hurry here anyway? Getting a postcard to California in less than five days is a religious experience to most of us. We use Federal Express when it absolutely, positively has to be there next week.

If you're hyperactive by nature, better move out east. You'd go nuts here. Quick-stop shopping is having a toll-free number to call in the back of the catalog. But we keep a sense of humor about it. We talk about all the other states. Everything that isn't Alaska is called "outside." That insinuates we're *inside*. Well, I wish they'd close the door. Cold in here.

We must move slower because its colder, like molasses. That, or we're just stupid. Probably a little of both. It's hard to tell. Things are expensive here. Maybe that's why we move slow; makes our money last longer. Of course, wages are high too. Maybe that's it. Might not be so stupid after all.

Alaskans are always asking each other how long they've been here. Longer the better. Do people in Indiana do that? I doubt it. Alaska's not as easy a place to live as some spots. I guess that's why there's honor in longevity. Could be we move slow because it isn't easy, and maybe we think a little more about it. I doubt it, but it sounds good. And besides, in the land of "different drummers," I'm just thankful mine beats a dull thud.

PART
6

DISTRACTIONS

Trivial Pursuit

OUR HOME and circle of friends have finally been infected with America's newest way to pass the time. Trivial Pursuit. The name implies the quest. The object of this game is to recall as many useless and often innocuous bits of information on a wide variety of subjects as possible. If you answer correctly enough times while your token is sitting on the right spaces on the game board, you'll win.

It's as easy as that, and more fun than a high school trig exam, if you think that's fun. In fact, I'm not sure they still teach trigonometry in high school, do they? Probably a question on that in here somewhere.

I'm sitting here surrounded by these little question-and-answer cards, and I'm getting in a bit of a dither. We had a late night in pursuit of this endless trivia last night, and by God, not all of these questions and answers make sense; in fact, some of them are dead wrong.

Listen to this one: "What is the only U. S. state to be free of houseflies?" Well, I don't know, but I'd guess it would have to be one separated from the contiguous United States somewhat, and Alaska's out because I can see about a pound of them bouncing off the window from here; so I say Hawaii. Wrong, they say Alaska.

I lost a turn on that one last night and I'm still hot about it. So what I'm gonna do is staple one of these big ol' black bugs to that particular card and send it to them postmarked Homer, Alaska. Now, I'm sure they'll write back smugly, just like your old geometry teacher used to look at you smugly when you missed a trick question, and tell me that, "Yes, there are in fact flies in Alaska. There are not, however, any of the species *House.*" Come on now. Let's be realistic here. Once a fly gets in your house, it's a housefly, right?

Here's another one that, though probably true, does not make any sense. "What is approaching when a cyclist shouts 'oil'?" A good guess would be that an oily spot on the road is approaching, right? Wrong. The answer is "car." What I want to know is why they would shout "oil" when a car is approaching, when they could just shout "car" and skip the interpreter. In fact, try yelling "oil" once or twice, then yell "car" a couple of times. It doesn't even take as much breath out of you to shout "car," and you'd think that would be important to a cyclist, but what do I know? Missed another turn.

Then right after a toughie like that, they'll slip you one like this: "What was the title of Mark Twain's autobiography?" You lie down on the rug clutching your temples, crying, "I know that, I know that!," and end up saying *Tom Sawyer* or something. The answer, of course, is *The Autobiography of Mark Twain.* So you learned something — two things, in fact. You learned the answer to a dumb question, and you also learned how far those little plastic game tokens will fly.

Here's another one missed that, had we been on a TV game show, would have been decided by the secret judges. "What is the world's fastest dog?" You see, there're two right answers to that one. If you were born in America before 1970 and have any fun in you whatsoever, you know that the world's fastest canine is UnderDog, fighting ever onward to rid us of that sinister little midget he was always chasing around while showing off for Sweet Polly Purebred. That was my wife's answer, and a darn good one too. But no, these stuffy, narrow-minded Canadians who make this game think that the world's fastest mutt is the greyhound. Big deal.

I get this image of the guys who write these questions and answers as the same guys who used to wear a lot of keys on their belts in high school and were always the ones who went to the audiovisual room to get the projectors and set them up. Boring people who we all thought would grow up to be janitors in large brick buildings, but instead they moved to Canada and invented this game. Talk about *Revenge of the Nerds;* this is it.

Here's one. "What do the Italians call Florence?" Probably looking for a nickname, so you say "Flo" or "Flossy." Nope, here they go and get cerebral on you again. "Firenze" is the answer. Who cares? Nobody slaps their forehead and goes, "Oh yeah!" when they hear that one. You just roll your eyes and stick the card back in the box. Your turn.

They've got several editions of this game. The one I have here is the "Genus" edition. I hope they never ask me what that means. It's the general edition for anybody born in this century, I think. Then there's the "Baby-Boomer" edition. There's a lot of television and Richard Nixon questions in that one. There's a "Sports" edition for folks who know a lot about that stuff. Like, "Who was the only golfer to win the U.S., British Opens, and Amateurs in the same year?" Probably the only person who knows the answer to that is the guy who did it. Then there's the "Silver Screen" edition for people who watch a lot of old movies and a few new ones. "What was the name of Sky King's niece?" Stuff like that.

I want them to make an edition for people who really don't care what the answers are. Questions like "What color is your hair?" or "How far is third base on a teenage date?" They'd make for a lot better table chatter than "What's the longest river in Asia?," don't you think?

I shouldn't be so hard on it. It is the first thing to come down the pike in a long time that's gotten Americans to actually talk to each other. There's probably good in that somewhere, and it is astonishing the amount of information we have stashed away in our brain buckets.

Say, "What was Beaver Cleaver's first name?"

New-Car Jitters

I REMEMBER when my folks would buy new cars. It didn't happen very often. In fact, I only can remember two times that they actually bought new ones. It was a real big deal for us. They'd pile all six of us kids in, and we'd go for a nice long drive. The first car was a station wagon. It was very impressive-looking to a little kid, downright awesome. That was in the days before middle-class guilt, and we could see that Mom and Dad were awful proud of the new wagon. They were in high spirits and would take turns driving while us kids would drop not-so-vague hints about stopping off at the Dairy Queen as long as we were out. Of course, the last thing they wanted was six sticky kids in the new car, but they'd stop.

It was kind of like a holiday. We'd marvel at the clean seats, while Dad would remark on the handling or pickup, and Mom would say how new cars always smelled so good. Boy, they sure did. I remember digging around under a seat for some reason and coming up with a glob of grease they must have forgotten to wipe off at the factory. It smelled like where that odor was coming from, and for the longest time I thought that was what it was for. Every new car must have a little glob of new car smell hidden away in it somewhere. When it didn't smell like a new car anymore, I thought it was because I had taken it out that day it was new. I never told anyone.

I was older when they got their other new one — to their severe discomfort, old enough to drive it. They'd read the mileage before I went out to be sure I wasn't out tooling around in the new car, which I usually was. But they'd keep letting me have it when I had a date. It hasn't been until very recently that I've begun to appreciate what a terrible sacrifice that must have been. We just got a new car ourselves. A little station wagon at that. It smells every bit as good as my folks' first new car did so many years ago. My wife and I took a nice long drive the day we got it, just like my folks used to. I commented on the handling and pickup while she said how new cars always smelled so good.

Well, the problem is that my dear old parents are going to be here for a visit next week, and we're going to loan them the car to get around in while they're here. At least that's the plan. You see, they aren't used to the way some of the roads can be around here, and I think we ought to take a mileage check on them to make sure they aren't off tooling around on any of the back roads, or goofing off with it. They aren't used to stick shifts anymore either, and I'd hate to think they were grinding the tips off

112

the virgin gears in our state-of-the-art Japanese transmission. Which brings me to another anxious thought. My dad is a strong believer in buying American products. He might not take kindly to a state-of-the-art Japanese automobile. Sabotage might not be out of the question.

Maybe they'll pay me back for breaking the drive line in their brand-new Pontiac Grand Safari so long ago. I was trying to lay rubber in all the wrong ways. At the time, I didn't realize that four-thousand-pound station wagons don't like to lay rubber. I'm sure they haven't forgotten about that. Or maybe they'll just go and have ice cream and leave the steering wheel all sticky. Parents'll do the darndest things sometimes.

I just don't know about this. They'd probably be much more comfortable in a big rented car made in Detroit. I'm just trying to make them feel at home. Besides, if they somehow found that little glob of new-car smell hidden away in there and took it with them, I just don't know what I'd do.

Soaps

I'M JUST A LITTLE embarrassed about this, but I've lost track of "All My Children." I couldn't help it. They just were beginning to disgust me a little. Erica is a stubborn, well, I can't say it but it rhymes with "rich." Nina is such a busybody, and Andrew was getting to be a regular ace wimp. So I let them go, all of them. I apologize to any of you who may be close with them, but I've traded them all in for new ones: Steve, Betsy, Craig, and Kim, Good old Dr. Bob, and the mysterious Michael Christopher. I'd been worried that Betsy never would find her way back to reality, but Diana has spilled the beans and most of Oakdale now knows that she's still alive but has amnesia and is in the twisted care of flaky Craig. Boy, I'd like to get him in a dark alley sometime. Steve is worried sick, and he and half the cast are over in Europe falling all over each other to find Steve's real father, who may hold

114

the key to our national security. I'm hooked and I have only the VCR to blame.

We can only program the VCR to record one show per day while we're at work, and choices must be made. "As the World Turns" so turn I. My wife and I started recording these soaps on a whim, and to offer a viewing alternative to some of the prime-time programming. We had to. One more bleeps and bloopers show and I'd have cracked. Soaps are pure and unpretentious. They don't throw out a one-liner and then stand there bobbing their heads around while the tape-recorded laughter clatters on. They don't play a lot of country music while they tear around in race cars leaving a trail of wrecked highway patrolmen in their wake. No. Soaps are just soaps. They talk to each other, yell a lot, miss their cues sometimes, and flub their lines. They act like perfect children half the time and lose their memories a lot, just like we do. I like these people.

Sometimes, when I get home, my wife will have already watched the day's episode.

"Frannie and Jay spent the night in the woods together," she'll say.

"Well, I'll be darned." I grin. "Did her dad find out?" I'll pull out the paper and relax a little. "Oh, by the way, how's Betsy?"

"She's fine, but her plastic surgeon fell in love with her and made her look like his ex-wife, who's dead, but she doesn't know the difference."

"Boy, Steve'll hit the ceiling when he hears about this," I think and go back to my paper.

I should feel sheepish about involving myself in the lives of these imaginary characters, but I don't somehow. I think it's great. These shows are like the light in the storm.

In fact, I think they even named one that, didn't they? Our lives can trudge on from one day to the next. We come and go, get happy, get hurt, get sick, grow old, and these folks in the soaps can eat lunch for a week. You can watch one episode where it ends with a guy leaving a party, miss three episodes, and find that on Friday that he hasn't made it to his car yet. I like that. If only life moved at that pace, we'd all live a long time. I guess we already do live a long time, but soaps make it seem a whole lot longer.

Laugh if you must, and watch your hot-rod show with talking cars that fly, or mercenaries that fire sixty-caliber automatic weapons from the hip while riding tandem on a dirt bike with a very large man with no hair, and then tell me how stupid the soaps are. Just be careful when you talk to me about my show unless you know what you're talking about. I know these people, and I believe in them. They're there every day, and they most always act the same. Kinda like family. So mind your own business.

Mailbox
Miracles

BOY, the stuff you get in the mail. Every day there's another ration of impersonal and often insulting letters. "Dear Occupant," "Dear Consumer" — the heck with that. If they haven't taken time to find out who I am, why should I bother with them? I even got one from a government agency addressed "Dear Waste Oil Generator." Come on now. It makes me sound like a piece of heavy equipment. I think they owe me an apology. There's only two kinds of junk mail I look forward to, free samples, and sweepstakes fliers.

I must have gotten six of those sweepstakes deals in one week. They come in all sizes, from ten million on down to a paltry hundred and fifty thousand. One more personal than the last. Very nice. They had my name plastered all over the certificates inside and a nice handwritten note from the president of the company explaining in no uncertain terms why I should not throw this stuff away.

Two million bucks, or eighty grand a year for life. A classic suburban dream home with blue shutters and real shrubbery. Sailboats, stocks and bonds, reflective beach walks, and red sports cars. Makes my heart fibrillate just thinking about it. Enter by March 1 and win a chance at this thirty-five-foot luxury motor home or a trip to Greece, your choice. What a gas.

The point of these things, of course, is to sell you magazines. But I didn't fall for their hard sell. No kidding. I really was just getting ready to order up a few when all this sweepstakes stuff came. So now I'm a real front runner the way I look at it, 'cause I've actually got a few magazine orders stuck to my entry form.

I took the time to sort through all that stuff and found all the secret stickers that qualify me for extra cash prizes and unimaginable luxuries like clock radios and pocket calculators. I got so many things stuck to my entry form it weighs a pound and a half. It took me all evening, and it's pretty gross. But by God, those suckers are going to go the distance. I can feel it.

I'm pretty optimistic about this whole business, as you can tell. I wanna have a washed-out picture of me on next year's sweepstakes envelopes. "You too can be a winner like your neighbor, Tom Bodett." I'll be standing in front of my thirty-five-foot luxury motor home on my way to Greece, my smiling family gathered around.

They say a person needs just three things to be truly happy in this world. Someone to love, something to do, and something to hope for. Well, I've already got someone to love, and filling in all this junk sure gives me something to do, and I hope to win like crazy. So between a good marriage and a post office box key, I've got a heck of a deal going here.

TV People

DID YOU EVER notice that nobody you see on television looks like anyone you know? They're all experiments in genetic engineering that couldn't find jobs doing anything else. They look and act exactly the same. If the women aren't cast as complete dingbats, then they've got them acting like Clint Eastwood in drag. Macho women detectives spend an hour yelling at everything in sight, then they'll portray a moment of tenderness or gender identification by sharing a lipstick in the ladies' room.

All the men look like the ace through king in the Chippendale card deck. To show character and a sense of humor, they put a baseball cap on them. Innocent boyish grins under the brim of a New York Yankees hat, and the hearts of America go pitter-patter.

They're all private detectives, too. I've never even met

a private detective. Can there really be that many? And do they all really look like that? I never see these kinds of people in airports or shopping centers. They don't work on my car, sell me groceries, give me parking tickets, or plow my road. Those folks look a lot like me. Sometimes our faces are dirty, our socks don't match, and our clothes get ripped. They don't rip provocatively at the shoulder or chest to show off anyone's manliness either. They rip right in the seat of the pants just before you walk into the coffee shop for lunch. I want to see more human beings being human.

Aren't you getting a little tired of eating hamburger casserole, trying to feel sorry for the poor young television heiress who's not getting her share of the oil revenues? Or how are we supposed to feel when our favorite private eye loses his wine cellar privileges, or wrecks the Ferrari when our cars sit in the driveway on bald tires? Not everyone in America's biggest problems are illegitimate children, terminal heart disease, and psychopathic killers, nor do they care to hear much about it. Most of us are dealing with high rents, boring jobs, and bunions. But what fun would it be to see that on the tube?

I can picture the network ads for a new drama set in Fargo, North Dakota. "Tune in Tuesday and share the excitement as Caroline gets a raise to minimum wage and Freddy surprises her with a matching set of vinyl dinette chairs." That series wouldn't last a week, would it? For good reason too, I suppose.

Maybe it's not so bad that we immerse ourselves in the fantasy worlds of the very rich and perpetually good-looking. As long as we don't all start thinking that the way they act is admirable behavior. I think the Freddys in Fargo who surprise their wives with tubular furniture are worth any ten of the vicious oil tycoons we so enjoy watching. I'd rather share a cup of coffee with my snow plow driver than almost anyone I've seen on TV since Ed Norton and Ralph Cramden.

That truck driver is kinda ugly, but by God, he sure is good people.

PART 7

THE OUTDOOR LIFE

Moose Hunting

OPENING DAY, 5:30 A.M., and the world is coming to life. People who haven't seen the predawn side of a Saturday for a year now are pulling on rubber boots, filling their magazines, polishing binoculars. Real outdoorsmen sit quietly waiting for the light. They know where they're going and how to get there. They don't talk about it and nobody knows where they are. Occasional sportsmen, like myself, joke nervously, trying to drive an old pickup truck quietly over a gravel road. Words curiously absent from our vocabularies pop up intentionally: "220 grain," "yearling," "game trail," "work the ridge." It all sounds good. We cradle good rifles as if they were extensions of ourselves, though we've just cleaned the dust out of the barrels the night before.

We hit the woods and, whether planned or not, everyone gets separated and stands alone in the quiet dawn.

That's when I remember why I like to hunt. It may appear to a casual observer that a man is just sitting on a stump staring at the forest. That's exactly what he's doing, but there's a whole world more than that. He's hunting, and that needs no justification. He may sit there all morning and do nothing more than eat a candy bar, but when someone asks him later what he's been up to, he won't say, "Well, I sat on a stump all morning and ate a Snickers." No, he'll say, "I went hunting." He didn't just walk the high ground to stay out of the muskeg and find a likely-looking stump to sit down on. Ask him. He worked the ridge up to the knoll overlooking the drainage and sat for a moose.

Did he see anything? Yes, he tried to grow antlers on a cow for over an hour as he watched the two floppy ears rotating like radar above the scrub willows. She finally got up, and right behind her two calves appeared out of nowhere and followed her casually out of the draw, vanishing into the brush. That's when he saw the other two hunters. A man and a boy. They were trying to walk carefully through the neck-deep willow but must have sounded like a drunk with the blind staggers to that cow and her calves.

The man on the stump ate his candy bar and watched the two walk past. The boy was bright-eyed and clutched his rifle in front of him as if the moose could shoot back and were likely to ambush at any momemt. He followed the man closely — his father, no doubt — and looked where he looked, stopped where he stopped. A magic day he'll never forget, moose or not.

He won't be the same after today. An early rite of manhood. Camping with the men. The dirty jokes he didn't always understand but committed to memory for the boys back at school. Seeing his dad with his friends, joking and laughing, and not apologizing for the language. Getting the nod, okay, when Uncle Joe offered him a beer. "But don't tell your mother," he said and winked. No, he's never going to forget this, the most important day in all of his thirteen years. "You pay attention," his dad says, "someday you'll be doing this on your own."

The man on the stump gets up and stretches, takes a deep breath, and walks back out to the road. He feels better for the effort and calls it a good hunt.

The father and son get back to camp and drink hot coffee. Over the ridge they hear a pickup clanking and squeaking its way out to the highway. "Beautiful day for a hunt," the father says.

And nobody heard a shot fired.

The Trapper

THERE WAS this old trapper I heard of. Nobody's seen him in years. He lives way up north of Circle someplace. Just him and his dogs. No one knows much about him other than his nearest neighbor, Tanner. That probably isn't his name, but that's what he does, so that's what everybody calls him.

Tanner would see the old trapper sometimes when he brought his skins to him. He never had much news and the old trapper had none, so they didn't ever talk much. The trapper would leave his skins and a list of supplies to trade for. Tanner would sell the skins in town, take his cut, and gather up the supplies on the list. Sooner or later the old trapper would show up, take his stuff, any leftover money, and disappear again.

A couple of shouts at the dog team and away he'd go

up the trail on his sled. Just him and his eight dogs. Those dogs were the only ones ever did hear that old trapper say much. That's why I don't know where this story comes from, but Tanner tells it and he ain't smart enough to make something up.

This old trapper works pretty hard, for a trapper any-way, and does okay by it. He's got himself quite a nice little log cabin he built, a few sheds and whatnot. He never buys anything but bullets, traps, and grub mostly. So he must have some little bit of money out there he don't care too much about.

There don't seem to be a whole lot he does care too much about except trapping, and it's hard to guess what he does out there all the time. He must hunt some, of course, moose and caribou mostly, sometimes bear. And he fishes, gotta fish. He's got piles of 'em froze solid and stacked like cordwood in one shed.

That's all he'll feed those dogs. Every night he makes a mean brew in an old fuel drum. The dogs yip and cry and hang against their lines when he starts dumping those froze fish in the boiling water. He throws 'em each some when it's good and warm, goes back in the cabin, and that's it. Except one night every year.

It's always at that time of year when the days are as dark as they're going to get. The lion's share of the trapping is still left to do and the coldest weather yet to come. It's those dark nights right around then he looks his dogs over closest. He checks their feet and mouths, feels their strong shoulders, and pats them on the rump.

He'd be sunk without those dogs. He knows that. Without them he couldn't go nowhere and couldn't take hardly nothing with him if he did. He couldn't live out there like he does without them, and it's during those bleak and darkest days he knows that best.

There's a night around then that's always different. He fires up the ol' fuel drum like usual, but instead of tossing in just a few fish, he drags out one big ol' moose leg and dumps it in there after he's hacked it up some with an ax. The dogs kind of coo and gurgle like huskies do when they smell stuff like that cooking. He gives them all a little more than he should and lets his lead dog in the cabin for the night to sleep by the fire just this once. He gives them all an extra pat on the rump in the morning and feels good about having them around.

Tanner tells this story every year over at the lodge on Christmas. He says it's a true Christmas story, but I don't know if it is, or if it even makes any difference.

The
Dog Fix

SPRING has a way of bring-
ing out the best in people and the worst in dogs. We're all
suddenly afflicted with a dose of energy that requires
proper channeling. People handle this with a minimum of
thought and effort. We get up earlier, maybe stay up later.
We clean a lot of garages. Dogs, on the other hand, can
only do what dogs will do; they run around a lot. In the
spring they just run farther and get there faster. This is how
my problem started.

He's a year-old, one-hundred-pound, brainless mass of
pure black Labrador. His marathon visits around the area
are well known and mostly tolerated by the neighbors. At
least until this spring speed-up began. Instead of his usual
practice of meandering between his girlfriends and sniffing
at the poultry, he's now leaving a swath of terrorized
bitches, children, and chickens in his wake. The neighbors

have of course let me know about this, and I'm certain the only reason he's still alive is that they've yet to draw a bead on him.

I had to make a decision whether to forcibly restrain him with chains and shackles, or try to teach him to just stay put. The former solution seemed too cruel and un-usual for a long-term remedy, and the latter is a little easier said than done.

Then there was a third remedy pointed out to me that I hadn't considered. "Why don't you have him fixed?" someone said. Even the sound of it made sense. Fixed, of course. If something isn't working right, you have it fixed. Off we went to Dr. Ralph's with fresh hope evident in our faces. Actually, I had hope; the dog just likes to ride in the truck.

I'm not exactly sure what castrating a dog is supposed to accomplish. They say it will relieve them of whatever hormones it is that make them run around from one friv-olous affair to the next, acting macho and showing off with the livestock. It wasn't without conscience, however, that I dropped him at the clinic to have this done. Feelings of treason to our gender seated themselves in my lower ab-domen as I left him victim to the dirty deed. I felt selfish and impetuous for not seeking a less surgical alternative, but soon justified it by the surety that life as a neuter would be much more rewarding for him than a thirty-cal-iber hollow point from an irate neighbor.

When they brought him back out to me at the clinic, I was stunned. The scene was reminiscent of that in *One Flew Over the Cuckoo's Nest* where Jack Nicholson is wheeled into the ward sporting a fresh frontal lobotomy. I thought, "What have I done to my dog?" He stood there blankly, giving just one uncomfortable wag of the tail when he finally recognized me. The vet assured me it was only the anesthesia and that it would wear off in a few hours. I showed him all over again how to get in the truck, where he promptly threw up on my tool box and peed on the seat. With a sense of having done a terrible wrong, I drove us home. He never looked at me.

The anesthesia did wear off, and I could soon see the one-year-old canine energy surging through him. I left him chained overnight for fear he'd wander off in his delirium and get hit by a truck, or join a religious cult. In the morning as I approached him he sat quivering with anticipation, bright-eyed and ready to go. All of my previous guilt vanished as I expectantly unhooked him to see what my newly rebuilt dog could do. I couldn't believe my eyes.

He took off in a series of about five high-speed figure-eights around the front yard. He had a look of manic glee about him as he dug in harder and faster on each pass. He finished off with a breakneck leap from the bank over the driveway, splaying his legs out sideways and knocking the breath out of him. He immediately began digging a hole at such a frenzied pace it would put a Case 580-D backhoe to shame. Then he sat in it and looked at me with a "What do you think of that?" look on his face.

I fell back against the doghouse in bewilderment. "Oh my God," I thought, "it's all gone wrong." He had all the same energy and drive, but no place to drive to. He's a ship without a wheel. A one-hundred-pound whirling dervish. I'd taken a perfectly normal and healthy young dog and turned him into the warmblooded equivalent of a "hot wheels" race car. I went back in the house and left him in his hole.

After some severe and effective soul-searching, I came to realize, "Well, at least he didn't leave the yard." I looked out at him and there he lay, peacefully sleeping, his empty head resting comfortably on huge paws. "Nothing wrong with that," I thought. "He'd have been halfway to Olsen Mountain by now, before yesterday." So I decided to go with it.

Of course the alleged hormones in question didn't disappear overnight. It's been a month now since I had him fixed, and he's run off a few times since then. He never goes far now, and it's usually just to check in and say hello to the old gang. I firmly believe he's a happier dog for all this. He spends less time on the chain, doesn't get disciplined much at all these days, and I take him down to the river to play a lot more. They say neutered dogs can get fat and lazy, so I'm more concerned for his health and exercise, and he likes that.

He still does his figure-eight stunt after being chained for a while, and I've even grown to enjoy that. Now when people come out to the house and say, "Hey, nice-looking dog," I just say, "Wait'll you see this." I unhook him, and as they stand there watching with a mixed look of awe and raw fear on their faces, I think, "That's my dog."

Halibut
Fishing

I HAD an old fishing friend call and ask if I wanted to crew with him for the halibut opening. For those of you who have never been involved with commercial halibut fishing, a little background might be in order. A halibut is a large, flat, bottom-dwelling fish. They swim flat-ways, but are built like they should be swimming upright, like real fish. Their eyes are about halfway in between the two positions as if they've been caught at an embarrassing moment in their evolution. I've often wondered how something as ugly as a halibut could taste so good.

Now, a halibut *opening* is when the Alaska Fish and Wildlife Department benevolently gives the fishermen three days a year to go out and catch as many of these critters as they can get their hooks on. After three sleepless days and nights, the fish are then brought back to town, where the canneries buy them at a price just slightly better than a poke in the eye with a sharp pike pole. Not being blessed with any better sense, I told my friend, "Sure, I'll go. Sounds like fun."

I knew right away there was going to be trouble when I saw we bought more bait than we did grub. By the end of the first day, however, the reason became evident as we spent a lot more time baiting hooks to feed the fish than we did feeding ourselves. The hooks are laid out on a large weighted bottom line at about twenty-foot intervals. These bottom lines are a mile long and longer, and it's no quick task to get one of these things in the water. Compounding the predicament is the fact that by the time you get one set baited and in the water, it's time to pick the last one up. So there's not much time to eat, but what's a little food when you're having fun?

As the first halibut approaches the rail, another problem arises: there are no handles on a halibut. For this they've devised a technical little jobber called a "gaff." A gaff is a steel hook with a handle on it which, when applied with a swift downward motion, will stick readily into a halibut's head, a boat's hull, or the operator's leg. Once the gaff is attached, the fish is then hauled over the rail and onto your lap, where it proceeds to thrash you to within an inch of your life. There is another handy little tool made explicitly for these occurences. That is an autographed Reggie Jackson Yankee Slugger hardball bat taped all the way to the label. This tool, when properly applied to the center of a halibut's head, will usually solve any further conflict.

Halibut, however, are one tough fish to kill. They've been known to flip defiantly and mess up your neatly squared-away hold pens after being gutted and iced overnight. For this reason a few extra whacks with the bat won't hurt anything. By the second or third day without sleep there is a tendency in some crewmen to beat the fish's head to the consistency of sandwich spread. This behavior should be encouraged, as it relieves tension on the boat and spoils the cheeks for the cannery, who won't pay for the heads anyway.

You can only have so much fun, and after three of these carefree days of fishing, you're forced to haul in the gear one last time and head to town. Now, there's no feeling in this world quite like pulling into town with your decks on the waterline and the bars still open. A couple hours of beer and lies with the other fishermen prepare you to proceed to the cannery to unload.

Another unforgettable experience is sending your hard-earned catch up to the dock, where they pay you half the price for the fish that you paid them for the bait that caught them. It doesn't take an accountant to feel a little chafed in the posterior over that.

All in all it's an experience one never forgets, hard as one tries. I'm still haunted by specters of cross-eyed flat fish in my sleep, and a wave of violent anger sweeps over me when the umpire yells "Batter up" at our league softball games. My land-lover hands are healing quite nicely, and I've gotten where I can actually resist recoiling in revulsion when I smell fish cooking.

King Salmon

ANOTHER eventful weekend in pursuit of the ever-elusive king salmon has come and gone. Like all foiled anglers, I dread the question that is ultimately asked when you say you've been fishing: "Did you catch anything?" Boy, I hate that. If I had caught anything, God knows you wouldn't have to ask me about it. More likely you'd have to tell me to be quiet.

I'm the last in a long line of frustrated fishermen. This is the guy who single-handedly stopped the 1977 pink salmon return in Southeast Alaska by simply getting a job on a seine boat. I've got a radio beacon hidden away in me somewhere that repels fish of all species within fifty miles. That doesn't explain why the guy next to me always gets a fish, but I think he cheats.

Anyway, I didn't get skunked this weekend, and if anyone asks if I caught anything, I can honestly say that, yes, I did. On Friday night I caught a cold. A nice one too. I caught a sharp stick in the face returning to camp in the dark. Caught my shirttail in my zipper several times, and also caught a hook in the shoulder while admiring the casting technique of an eight-year-old kid. This might sound like a real fish story, but that's not all. I caught hell when I got home, and even my wife got something. She caught a plane back east to spend some time with her family until this whole king salmon thing blows over.

I'm making myself out to be a fairly inept fisherman, but that really isn't the case. Actually, I have very tight control over things. For instance, I can control the angle of the sun in relation to the good fishing holes by leaving my sunglasses in the truck. I can cause the temperature to plummet as much as twenty degrees in just a few hours by forgetting to wear my longjohns. Rain control is the easiest. I can make it stop and start and stop and start by putting my jacket on and taking it off, putting it on and taking it off. Why don't I just stay home? you're probably asking yourself. Well, that's pretty obvious. All that rain and cold weather was ruining the garden. Besides, I'd miss the beauty of it all.

Picture five hundred shimmering "spin-'n'-glows" being applied in a captivating rhythm. The resounding cries of "Fish on" every time someone hooks the line of the guy across the river. Glistening globs of monofilament line wafting gently down the current and, most colorful of all, the language of the guy who snarled it up. How could I stay away?

You learn things on the river. You learn that RVs really have people in them. You meet all kinds of folks from such interesting, faraway places as Elmendorf and Muncie. Fishing for the king salmon on a wild Alaska river is something that most people only get to dream about. I feel fortunate to be able to realize that dream, and also share it with several hundred other dreamers crammed into a half-mile stretch of riverbank.

Hollywood
Discovers
Alaska

I SAW an unnerving headline in the paper not long ago: "Hollywood Discovers Alaska." I went cold wondering if they'd do for us what they did for doctors, policemen, and cowboys. Put us on some pedestal of superhype that we could never live up to. Portray some massive concept of character and place that would trigger a statewide identity crisis. I pictured throngs of Alaskans lined up outside our state mental health clinics complaining, "We're good, but not *that* good!"

That fear subsided, however, as I read the article and realized what they were really up to. It seems one big movie outfit is up at Barrow making a Santa Claus flick. That seems harmless and wholesome enough by itself, but the plot of the thing has our oil companies trying to take over the North Pole or something. Well, oil is to Alaska what corn is to Iowa; that's our *stuff.* It fuels our state economy, builds our roads, and offers a lot of jobs to a lot of people. So what this movie is doing is showing us Alaskans messing around with Jolly Saint Nick over a little oil field and putting us alongside such infamous Christmas demons as the Grinch and Scrooge. Come on now. We have kids too. We wouldn't monkey with Santa, honest.

It occurs to me that Hollywood isn't interested in inflating our image at all. They're after something altogether different.

Another big movie company went to work outside of Anchorage. A story about two escaped convicts who get away on a train that somehow becomes a runaway. It goes from there with a lot of large dangerous machinery moving at high speeds through scenic winter settings, I suppose. Your normal high-production adventure film.

Getting behind the spirit of the thing, the state-owned railroad even offered use of their equipment for the train scenes. So the first thing the director wants to do is repaint the engines. "Not sinister enough," he said. The bright blue and gold colors of our state flag were replaced by a morose wash of unscrupulous black paint. Oh, they'd restore them to their original color scheme when they were done, all right, but first they must make sure they capture the inherent evil here. After all, this is Alaska, land of the fiends and home of the depraved.

Boy, I don't think I like the way we're coming across down there. To listen to the media, you'd think all we did was hunt elves and reindeer to get more oil revenue and afford more efficient means of exterminating wolves. Come on now. I've never even seen an elf.

I'm afraid that this kind of negative publicity is going to attract the wrong type of people to our state. Moral slummers who need a few weeks of a good red-meat-and-smashed-potatoes sort of experience. Then I hear that Tom Selleck of TV fame is over on Kodiak Island for a bear hunt, and see that it's already started. We've become chic. A mecca for those that need to reassociate with their primal tendencies. Some less than honorable entrepreneurs might well take advantage of this trend. I can see it all now.

"Wanna kill something? Come on up! That's about all we do here. Sign up for one of our environment-trashing weekend package tours. We got lots of environment. Bring your own trash, or use ours. No extra charge."

"Endangered species, my eye! We'll show 'em endangered with one of our Jet Ranger high-altitude bald eagle roundups." Or try a "See how drunk you can get and still kill a mountain goat" hunting adventure. We aim to please, so you aim too, please. We want everybody back home safe and sound to brag us up and get your friends up here next year.

Tell them how we got so much wildlife they can run into it with their cars if they want, or take the deluxe route and shoot at it from airplanes. Of course, you won't have to convince them of the deliciously evil and irresponsible people we have around here. They've already seen that in the movies.